CREATIVE PAPER TOYS & CRAFTS

Michael Grater

Illustrated by the Author
Photographs by John Hunnex

DOVER PUBLICATIONS, INC.
NEW YORK

Published in Canada by General Publishing Company, Ltd.,
30 Lesmill Road, Don Mills, Toronto, Ontario.
Published in the United Kingdom by Constable and Company, Ltd.

This Dover edition, first published in 1981, is a slightly altered re-
publication of the work first published in 1972 by Mills & Boon
Limited, London, and Taplinger Publishing Company, New York,
under the title *Paper Play*. For the Dover edition the original Acknowl-
edgements and Note to American Readers have been eliminated. Of the
original eight pages in color, five have been reproduced in black and
white and three have been omitted because they duplicated other
illustrations.

International Standard Book Number: 0-486-24184-X
Library of Congress Catalog Card Number: 81-67087

Manufactured in the United States of America
Dover Publications, Inc.
180 Varick Street
New York, N.Y. 10014

CONTENTS

Introduction   This book can be read through from cover to cover, or it can be dipped into at will. It is about some of the ways we can use a simple and exciting material—paper.

Playing—and there are many opportunities for this suggested in the following pages—is not just a time passing activity of no importance. People play games—some of them with great skill—or they play musical instruments. We can play in our own way at a very early age, or we can play when we are very old. Playing is fun, and the more we do it the more we learn about something.

In this book about paper—and about card—there are suggestions for the beginner and there are also suggestions for those who are older and more experienced. There are opportunities for those who can play freely and are happy to make wild experiments. There are also suggestions for those who are more precise, for those perhaps who incline towards accuracy and mathematical developments, rather than to free and unpredictable experiments.

We are all of us surrounded by shapes and colours, and these are changing all the time. This is our world and it is important for us as individuals to see what is around us and what is happening to it. To develop this ability we can participate in many practical ways in the materials of the modern world, exercising our hands and our eyes.

One of the simplest of these materials is paper. It is simple but it is extensive. It is everywhere. It is used for communication between us. It wraps our food and the things we need. It is plain, coloured, striped, spotted, textured, smooth, large, small, thick, thin, expensive, cheap. It is used by everyone, because it cuts, folds and sticks easily. And it is easy to get.

For any of the suggestions made in the following pages there are no special requirements. Papers and cards as they come, salvaged or bought in local stores; a pair of scissors, a knife if possible, impact adhesive and colours to decorate some of the work—these are the things we need.

None of the suggestions has to be slavishly copied. They are all included and described as starting points or as descriptive examples of techniques. In some instances diagrams have been included for the benefit of some readers. Others will not need them.

Many of the earlier exercises are suggested as hanging opportunities, but this is because paper is light and unless it is made up into more solid forms, the mobile is one of the best ways of keeping the finished work safe.

Much of the early work is about shape, and this is because we need to know about it if we are going to use it. We are surrounded by shapes—in nature in all its different aspects, and through the efforts of the architects and planners who work on our environment.

When we take up a piece of paper it has a shape, and when we fold it or cut it we make a shape. This is what paper play is about—folding and cutting. It is for any one of us at almost any age. And it is about shapes, how we can make them, and how we can use them. In particular it is about some of the very many ways we can enjoy a simple material—and about some of the fun and satisfaction we can get as, young or old, we take up a piece of paper and begin to play with it.

Paper

Paper is a simple material, and anyone who reads this book, either straight through from beginning to end or here and there in the parts which happen to be interesting, should without much difficulty find some suitable material to begin with. It might be white or coloured, plain or decorated, from a parcel wrapping or from an exercise book. There is no special sort of paper which has to be used. If we want to develop the beginnings of a skill in handling the material we must be prepared to cut and experiment, and we must not be too worried at this stage about special art papers or fine quality cards. There is plenty of paper around us, and there is a lot of it we can use as we work.

It does not matter how many of us in any part of the world are actually reading this at this moment and are thinking about playing with paper, and it does not matter how many different sorts of paper are going to be used as starting points for any of the work suggested; the single common factor between all of us will probably be that we are all starting with paper in a particular shape. Most of us will have paper which, regardless of its source or quality, is rectangular like this page.

This is obviously because paper is a material which can be cut easily along a straight edge and which is convenient to handle in a simple shape with neatly ordered and straight sides. But this common factor gives us a useful starting point. The rectangle or square can be cut or manipulated into any number of new and different shapes. As we work there will often be little similarity in our discoveries, but the starting point can be a shape we all know, so that we can set off from the same source to explore and develop a whole range of possibilities in the material. In this process we might discover that paper has as much play potential as some of the most special and expensive sorts of toys.

As a common starting point we can begin with the special sort of rectangle—the square (Fig. 1). This is a shape which we are all taught about at school so that most of us, when we look at it, will know something about it—about the sides and their relationship and about the angles. But for our purpose our concern must be with what the shape looks like and what we can do with it.

Fig. 1 Start with a familiar shape.

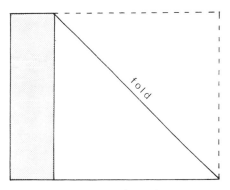

Fig. 2 From a rectangle to the square.

If we start with a rectangle it will, of course, be possible to make a square by measuring along the length and down the sides, making them all equal before we cut. We can also make a square from a rectangle by folding the paper in two on a diagonal, so that one of the sides matches with the bottom of the paper. The folded triangle will be one half of the square, and any extra paper—toned portion Fig. 2—can be cut away from the original rectangle.

The square which we are starting with can be treated in many ways to change its appearance. It can be crumpled, for example, into a ball. But when we work with paper or with any material we must obviously make the things we do more deliberate than this. Although we intend to play with the material, we should try to control it and make it work for us.

If we consider what we can do with this square of paper we will see that we can either alter its shape by cutting, or we can work on the surface and change its appearance in a different way (Fig. 3).

Fig. 3 The shape can be altered in various ways.

But there are so many different ways in which we can do either of these things. In the first case we can cut any or all of the sides, or the corners, and our cuts can be straight or curved. If we work on the surface we can use pencils, pens felt-tips, crayons, paints or dyes. We can make resist treatments with wax; we can print or we can make collages of other materials. We can put on textures, patterns, shapes, colours and tones. And everything we do to this shape, regardless of what we have been taught about it, will alter its appearance.

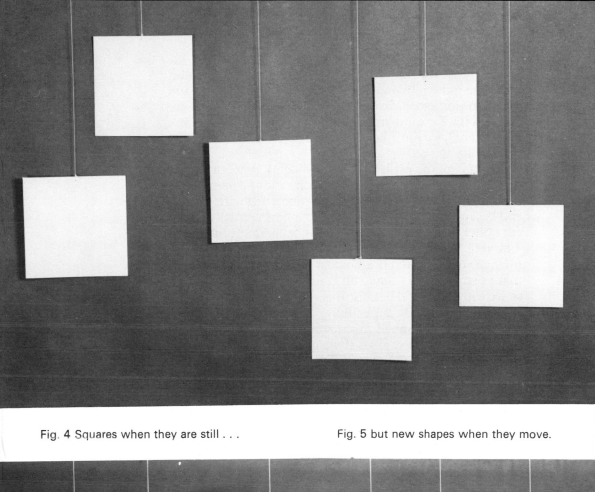

Fig. 4 Squares when they are still . . .   Fig. 5 but new shapes when they move.

In any treatment of the square, even at the simplest level, we must rely on our eyes. The ability to select and decide on different treatments will be based on what we see, and if we want to make progress in the way we can use the material, we must be prepared or even keen to exercise this ability to see.

In many of the earlier exercises which follow, the treatments suggested are measured or geometric and predictable rather than freely inspired. We are concerned with shapes, and because we will be using paper our concern will be with cut rather than drawn shapes. This is deliberately intended. The ability to draw is a special skill which might be difficult for some of us. Also at the moment we are not setting out to make pictures. We want to find out something about paper so we will cut it. And because it is very light in weight some of the things we cut can be hung up. If we make pictures they are usually pinned to the wall. We can do this with some of our early exercises if we like, but we can also use the space above us. We are setting out to discover some of the ways in which paper can be manipulated, and to do this we must learn to look at shapes.

If we cut a number of squares of paper or card and hang them from their top centre point (Fig. 4) we will find, if we let them hang freely and if we do nothing more to them, that each square will change in appearance as it moves (Fig. 5). And this change will continue as we go on looking at the shape. The two illustrations are of the same thing seen differently. In Fig. 5 the square we started with makes new shapes because the material is light and we can suspend it. This is a simple but important fact in our understanding of the material. We might know what a square really is, but more important to us is what it looks like when it is treated in certain ways. As a shape our common starting point has much potential.

Much has been written recently about shapes, about where we can look for them and how we can find new ones by using our eyes. Many of us will have had some opportunity to work with shapes in drawing or craft lessons. We might have cut vegetables and looked at the cross section. We might have been encouraged to discover and draw new shapes from our everyday surroundings, because it is important for us to learn how to respond to our world by using our senses as fully as possible. Since we are surrounded by shapes we might, in the early stages of our work with paper, set up some simple experiments or exercises which will make us look at shapes and which will later help us to make decisions as we work.

Shape on Shape

We have seen that the square can be made to change its appearance by hanging it so that it moves. Starting again with this known shape we can affect its appearance by other treatments. We can place other shapes on it.

In Fig. 6 the same square has different shapes placed on it. In this exercise it is not necessary to cut the shapes as shown. It is a looking, not a making exercise.

In this very simple visual statement we can see that a shape placed on another shape has a very different visual effect according to its size. In the first row, the small square at the top and the largest square at the bottom can be compared. It is interesting to isolate these two shapes by covering the rest of the examples. When we apply shape to shape we can work large or we can work small, and there will be very pronounced visual differences in the same way that there will be visual differences if we put another shape on the square, like the circles illustrated.

There are, of course, no rules to tell us which is the right shape when we cut paper, but we are not setting out to learn rules. We are playing with shapes so that we can learn something about them.

If we can think of cutting and hanging a square we can see that, as well as changing its own appearance as it moves, we can apply other shapes which will also change. A simple exercise would be to cut a square, and then to put a small square of contrasting colour on one side and a large square of the same colour on the other. It could be a useful exercise in measuring and cutting, but more important—if we are really interested enough to hang it and look—it will tell us something about putting one shape on another.

In the shape on shape illustration, the first row has squares on our original square because we are starting from something we all know. Our next step forward must be into different shapes but we might control the pace of our experiments in these early exercises.

As we are familiar with the square we are all familiar

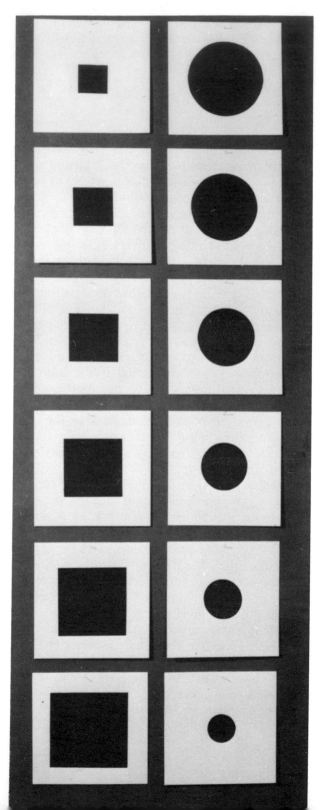

Fig. 6 Shape on shape
—the effect of size.

with the circle which is another basic and easily recognized shape. To cut circles in paper—and we will need many of them for later exercises—we will need to draw with a pair of compasses or we will have to rely on drawing round any available circular shape. It will probably be necessary to practise cutting on the drawn line until we can produce an adequate circular shape, but we can combine practice with some of the exercises.

It might be interesting, since our concern is with shapes, to discover if we do not already know it, the best shape to start with if we want to make a circle. If we start with a square again and find the centre point by crossing the diagonals we can construct the circle, and we can see (Fig. 7) how closely the two are related visually. If we refer back to Fig. 6 we can see what would happen if the arrangement of circles on the square continued upwards through two or three more examples. We would arrive eventually at something like the shape shown here.

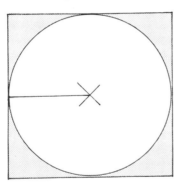

Fig. 7 Relating shape to shape.

Fig. 8 The placing of shape on shape can be important.

The placing of a shape on another shape is also important. In Fig. 8 the black squares are the same size and they are on identical backgrounds. But their different placing creates new shapes. We can learn from this to look carefully at both applied shapes and at their backgrounds as we work.

If the placing of a single shape on a background allows us to make or find new shapes, as we decide on its positioning we can extend the potential by repeating a shape on the background. The circles (Fig. 9) are cut as three discs of white paper and three of black in related sizes.

Repeating Shapes 1

Fig. 9 Similar shapes can be visually different.

When they are placed together in the first arrangement the discs are concentric, each of them having the same central point, but the placing is varied in the other examples and the visual effect is entirely changed.

This could be a useful starting exercise for anyone really interested in shape. Cutting the circles, the largest of which could be made to fit the width of this page would be good practice with the scissors, and we could learn from playing with the circles. How many different ways are there of arranging the six circles, and how many different shapes can be discoverd between them?

In Fig. 10 the same treatment is applied to our original shape. In this case the six squares are cut and examined in various arrangements. As an exercise these can again be cut in contrasting black and white and should be in related sizes, for example: from 6 inches down to 1 inch, or from 12 down to 2 centimetres (reducing each time by 2 cm).

Fig. 10 Shapes on shape will create new patterns.

The five separate units in the illustration include in each case all six squares. If the squares are measured and cut they can be used as a simple arrangement game. How many different ways are there of putting these six squares together? And what can we learn from the activity if we try it?

When we cut and place shapes on shapes we are working decoratively, and when we are using our hands and eyes together the exercises add to the skill we are developing personally.

After trying this sort of exercise we will have discovered that it requires care rather than any special sort of gift to work in this simple way with paper, but if we have been able to achieve some of the different visual possibilities of the arrangements of squares or circles we will have come a long way from the crumpled paper ball situation.

At this point in our work we are beginning to look perhaps a little more closely at some of the shapes we normally take for granted. Since we are working from recognizable geometric beginnings we might find that we are looking more closely at man-made works rather than at the less precise shapes of nature, but the important thing at this stage is to be looking. The shapes in a modern building and their various arrangements might mean more to us after we have tried any of these simple opportunities for playing with squares than they did previously.

In any of our work with paper we will be concerned with shapes and their arrangement—in a fun face, or as stripes on a tail—and wherever we go with our eyes open we will be close to shapes in various arrangements. The processes are linked. We must use our eyes as we work, and at the same time we can develop a simple but convincing ability to use shapes ourselves. In any craft there must be certain basic skills, and the potential skill in the craftsman's hands is closely related to the way he can use his eyes.

We can go to school to learn about a shape but there is probably a lot more we can find out about it for ourselves.

If we start again with the familiar square we can this time, instead of considering how it can be manipulated with other shapes, consider it as a shape which has a great deal of potential in itself.

Most of the work we attempt later will include many sorts of papers in differently cut shapes. We can of course, sit down at any time and cut shapes in paper, but we might be helped in the later exercises if we spend a few minutes considering how shapes can be discovered and used deliberately.

If we start once again with the square as the shape we all know, we can find new shapes by cutting and rearranging it. The top square in Fig. 11 is disguised in a number of different ways in the rest of the illustration. In each case nothing is added and nothing is taken away. The square is simply cut and the pieces rearranged.

The Rearrangement of Shape

Fig. 11 A shape can be cut and rearranged.

In the example immediately beneath the square, the two triangles placed point to point are the result of cutting the square through the diagonal.

In the shape underneath this these triangles are cut again through the centre and turned to make another arrangement. It is an interesting and not too demanding exercise to cut a number of quite small squares and to cut and rearrange each of them without adding or removing any part of the original.

We can try this as an exercise in simple mobiles. The mobile is a piece of art or craft work which relies for some of its effect on movement. There are various ways of making the movement possible, but the simplest of these is that of hanging the work.

The decorated squares in Fig. 12 are all examples of the square with another square applied to it, but in this case the applied square has been cut and rearranged on the background. The original two squares are shown in the shape on the left, and the others are all developments from this beginning.

Fig. 12 Shape on shape has many possible variations.

It is interesting to look at the two examples closest to the original. They both have the same four black squares, but the simple difference in their placing makes the final effect quite different.

A number of simple mobiles like this, in black and white which is a very strong contrast—or in any other combination of colours—can be quite pleasing if they are hung in a suitable place. They are perhaps too stark and serious for a bedroom, and there are in any case many more light-hearted opportunities in later exercises. But they might be interesting in a classroom, especially in one where work on shape and area and perhaps some simple geometry have already been started. The mobile shapes must of course be decorated on both sides, although not necessarily with the same treatment. If the applied shapes on one side are seen as the positive shapes, and the backgrounds they make as the negatives, the positives and negatives might be reversed on the other side. It would be a simple but useful exercise not only in cutting and sticking, but also in looking.

Even more important than this will be the fact that the mobiles will be examples of original research. We will be experimenting and making our own discoveries. The illustrated examples are only a few of the very many different ways in which a square may be cut and rearranged on another slightly larger one.

If we can find a place to hang this exercise we will now know also that the shapes we have made will go on changing after the squares are hung, making new shapes of their own. In this and in any creative exercise there are two important processes involved. Firstly, there is the process of doing something and watching a piece of work take shape. After this there is the further process of looking and looking again at the finished work. We can go on enjoying it, and we can go on making new discoveries from it.

It is quite usual, when we make pictures, for us to put them on the wall. There can hardly be any real reason for not extending this so that we have around us some visually exciting—but actually moving—pieces of work. In later pages there are many more opportunities for hanging as well as for free-standing objects which we might make in paper or card, but it would be a pity at this early stage not to try some of the simplest exercises like these rearranged squares. We must learn from doing them, even if we do not find it easy to state exactly what it is we have learned.

Fig. 13 Combined shapes can be contrasted.

The cutting and rearrangement of squares suggested in this exercise is only one of many opportunities we have for simple mobiles. The squares could have been placed on different background shapes, on circles or on triangles. Would this, in fact, be possible? Or would it be more difficult? We might have to try it to answer these questions.

A hint of the potential can be seen by comparing the squares in Fig. 13 with those in Fig. 12. In this illustration the same background shape, the square, is treated with an exploration of the circle, again cut and rearranged in various ways. The positive or applied shapes again make interesting and new negative shapes, some of which might be quite familiar—for example: the third from the top, which is probably not an entirely unknown shape.

Shapes are in some ways a little bit like words. The dictionary of shapes will never be compiled, but we can learn to use them and to extend our own personal vocabulary of shapes as we cut and arrange paper, and especially as we look at the results.

It is not necessary to describe in words the shapes we find. This would only confuse. What we must try to do is to learn how to find and make new shapes so that we can extend the scope of our work. Even at this early stage we might have already discovered something exciting about the squares and circles we normally take for granted in our everyday experience of the things around us. It is fun to experiment and discover, and as far as shapes are concerned we do in fact spend all of our waking lives looking at them.

Colour and Shape

Most of us have had some opportunity to work with colours. The opportunity to crayon or paint is something we grow up with, and there can be very few of us who have never painted a picture or a pattern.

At this moment, being concerned with shapes and their arrangement or rearrangement, we are concerned with pattern. We have seen how this can begin to be developed on a surface by cutting and applying new shapes. We can also use these shapes as starting points for work with colour.

If we take paints and paper and start to paint a pattern there are many ways of going about it. We can start merely by doodling, by making haphazard marks on the paper and then working from these to new marks. Or we can use deliberate pattern-making techniques. We can load a brush with colour and we can take a line for a walk with it —wherever we please across the picture space. Or we can look at something and discover shapes which we can borrow and use for our own purposes. The inside of a fruit or vegetable suggested earlier will make an interesting starting point, or we might use something we have picked up on a beach. When we put shapes on paper to make patterns we need a starting point. It does not just happen. Those of us who have been taught in one way will have looked closely at many different natural and man-made objects. We might have used magnifying lenses and we might have enlarged small details of seen shapes into large and exciting patterns. If we have worked with colours and tones we will have learned about them, not everything that there is to know, but in our own way something of their potential and how they can be used for visual effect.

When we work with cut and applied shapes, now and in later exercises, we can discover new opportunities for experiment and statement with colour.

In Fig. 14 the hanging squares of previous exercises, with cut shapes applied to them, have been extended into a new activity. In this case pen and brush work has been included. In the first example a circle has been cut through the diameter and rearranged on the background square. The negative shape has then been treated with a pattern of drawn lines instead of being left blank.

In the next example the semicircles are cut again and rearranged differently. They are then used as a starting point for more applied colour. The use of colour in any exercises with cut shapes can be fun. When we paint we usually do it for pleasure. It is a form of play. But we need shapes to put our colours in, and we can be helped by having guides which will lead us on to new experiments.

Each of the mobiles in the illustration (Fig. 14) starts with a shape we know. In each case this shape has another familiar shape cut and rearranged on it. In some cases the applied shape is cut from decorative wrapping paper. The applied shapes are then used as a guide for further painted experiment.

The use of decorative wrapping papers which occurs in this exercise will be seen again in many subsequent illustrations. These papers which are available in a wide

Fig. 14 Pattern experiment can be developed with shape on shape.

variety of colours and patterns are exciting to use, and their use is an aspect of our work with paper. They are often bright and excellent in colour, and the designs printed on them make them a pleasure to use. Their use in any of our work does not have to be considered as being better or worse than a hand-painted surface treatment. It is merely different. We can collect and save patterned papers to use sometimes in our work, and at other times we will make our own patterned surfaces. The printed papers, which can often be salvaged at no cost from parcel wrappings, only add to the possibilities open to us. When we see these in stores now we might look at the patterns with a different point of view, disregarding them perhaps as wrapping papers and wondering instead whether or not they will add to the decorative quality of our own work in paper.

26   The serpent in Fig. 15 has some painted pattern and some shapes cut from gift wrappings as part of its decoration. It started out as an exercise in measured rectangles, and when it was decided to put them together in this shape, a spotted pattern was chosen for the surface treatment, although some of the spots turned out to be rather larger circles. Some of these were cut from plain and some from patterned papers, and they were used as starting points for further painted treatment.

Fig. 15 Measured shapes with applied decoration can take many forms.

The serpent was then arranged in various ways on various background areas—sometimes long and straight as though it was stretched out, and sometimes curved or, as in the illustration, making new shapes. This was an exercise in measuring and cutting which was extended into a creative opportunity with colour and pattern. It is included here because we might now be ready to apply some of our shape and pattern experience into new and exciting opportunities.

If we look at the way a number of decorated rectangles make a sort of serpent, we could visualize perhaps a caterpillar made up of a series of decorated circles put together. It could be a striped caterpillar or a spotted caterpillar. It could be a blue one, or a green and yellow one. It could start at the classroom door and wriggle its way along the corridor wall, or we might have a smaller one somewhere in the bedroom—brightly coloured and attractive.

Fig. 16 Pattern making can be tried on experimental shapes.

If we are not too happy about serpents and caterpillars we can still combine shapes with colours to make new and interesting visual effect.

For example, we might take a few sheets of paper. In the exercise illustrated three sheets were used. The pattern started as three familiar shapes. But each sheet was cut into three long thin rectangles along its length. Each of the rectangles was then folded into four and, while still folded, was cut at the outer edges into simple familiar shapes.

The shapes were then opened out flat to make the chains shown. These were then used as a starting point for pattern painting (Fig. 16). In the illustration the results are shown displayed vertically on a wall in a close arrangement. This is a simple and adequate arrangement, remembering that the paper started as the familiar rectangle which we are used to displaying on the wall. But there are other possibilities.

If we turn the page sideways we will see the shapes and patterns differently. If we can make some simple cut patterns for ourselves—it might even be possible to persuade a group of friends to work together in a school—we might try any number of different arrangements. We might try meeting the shapes at the centre like the spokes of a wheel, or we might try a zig-zag arrangement. We might also try putting a face on one end, so that the result would be like a group of thin people in patterned shirts. Or if we put faces on the shapes and turned them sideways they might seem like caterpillars again. It might be interesting, if the head was on the end of the shape, to fix it with all the rest on the ceiling, as though they were walking across the room (Fig. 17). It would at least be a different way of showing and seeing the result. And we did start from a different sort of beginning.

If we could cut the shapes and then pattern them on both sides we could hang them so that they moved gently in the breeze and made new patterns. We could make an effect by using a single colour throughout, mixing tones with the addition of black or white, or we could use any other combination of colours. In each case the effect would be different. Some of our friends might like the result, others might not. But we would not know unless we were prepared to try it.

Fig. 17 Crawler with patterned shapes.

This exercise is an example of one of the many ways we can use shape in our work with paper. In this case, as a result of folding the paper we are using repeating shapes as a start to further pattern and colour work.

Repeating Shapes 2

When we folded and cut the long rectangles in the previous exercise we were trying a slightly unusual method of working on paper. It is much more usual to start and to go on working on a rectangle. But there is no rule which says we must do this, and we might have enjoyed the new experience of working on these repeated shapes.

The repetition of shapes is specially suitable to our work at this stage because we are cutting rather than drawing, and with many types of paper it is easy, by folding, to cut a number of similar shapes at the same time. The arrangement of repeated shapes into new patterns might interest some of us as we work.

Fig. 18 Any arrangement of shapes . . .

Fig. 19 . . . can be instantly changed.

In Fig. 18 the simple horizontal arrangement of circles —or vertical arrangement if we turn the page sideways— changes dramatically when the placing is slightly staggered, and more so when a new shape is added to each circle (Fig. 19).

It is interesting to consider how many different arrangements of the six circles with their inset squares might be possible if we played a finding-out game with them. If we cut the shapes out—or any other shapes we might like to experiment with—we can move them around on the working surface. It is a way of discovering patterns—not in our head, but actually by doing and looking. It is much better to work with cut-out shapes then with drawings of shapes. Drawing would take much more time to do, and it would in any case depend entirely on our ability to draw exactly and accurately the shapes we wanted.

By moving shapes around we learn about them. In Fig. 20 there is an arrangement of six triangles with applied semicircles. In this arrangement the triangles are in a straight vertical, making a new shape like a Christmas tree.

In Fig. 21 a different arrangement of the same shapes starts to produce a curve. In this instance each triangle is placed at the same point against the side of its neighbour, and a curve develops this time instead of a straight arrangement. It might be interesting to cut some shapes like this and to think about why we get a curve instead of a straight, or whether we might be able to use the discovery in our later work.

Fig. 20 Shapes in one arrangement . . .

Fig. 21 . . . make new shapes in another.

Discovering Shapes

As we cut paper and as we play with shapes we are developing the hand and eye skill which will help us to work more confidently in later experiments. We have already seen the beginning of the way shapes can be made to work for us, and that we can use simple rather than complex and difficult shapes in many different ways.

If we take a familiar shape again, and if we cut part of it away we will get new shapes. There are thousands of new ones we can find by cutting the familiar square or circle, but we might now begin to exercise some control on the cuts we make. Snipping at paper for fun is a way of occupying time, fun for some people perhaps, but it is interesting to consider how we can cut shapes deliberately. We will need them in later exercises.

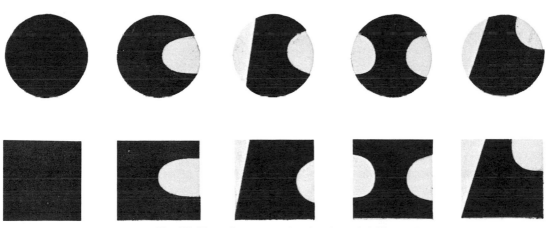

Fig. 22 New shapes can be developed deliberately.

In Fig. 22 a circle and a square are used as starting points. If we look from left to right we can see how each new shape is made from the first. In the first one a curved or concave section is removed. In the next one this happens again, but this time the shape also has a sloping cut on its side. In the second example from the right at the bottom we have a shape which we have seen before in a previous and different exercise, and in the one above this we have a shape which we will use later (Fig. 44). All of the shapes are made by cutting away a part of the original, and there are many shapes we can make in this way—by cutting and by knowing what sort of cuts we have used.

Fig. 23 Discovered shapes can be put together in different ways.

The vertical and curved arrangements of repeated shapes (Fig. 23) are examples of multiple arrangements which can now be traced back to a source. Both of the shapes occur in Fig. 22 as cut developments from the original square or circle. By comparing them we can see how the shapes were decided on, and what happens in one of the many arrangements possible.

The notes on these illustrations have been deliberately brief because, although there is a lot to be considered when we work with shape, it is in the end less important to read about it than to look at shapes and to consider how they can be discovered and used.

We are going to use lots of shapes in the future, and we will be cutting up a lot of paper and card. Every time we cut we will be making a shape, and we will be helped in our work by knowing a little about some of the processes involved, or better still about some of the opportunities which we might discover in a rectangle or square of paper.

Shape and Movement

We have already seen that when we are working in paper we are working in a lightweight material. If we appreciate this we will treat the paper properly. It is not strong and it is not easy to construct it into large and complicated works. It is light and it moves easily. We can demonstrate this, or get a feeling for it, if we take up any piece of fairly thin paper between finger and thumb and if we move our hand gently from side to side. As we make the movement the paper will waft gently against the normal air pressure, and will make subtle and changing curved shapes of its own. We can now begin to exploit this lightness in a range of new work. To begin with we can learn about the mobile or hanging shape, and we can discover ways of controlling and using the lightweight factor in paper.

In Fig. 5 we saw that shapes hung up so that they will move will make new shapes. We should begin to realize now that there are many different shapes we can hang, and as many different ways of treating the surfaces of these shapes as there are different ways of making paintings. We can use bright or dull colours; we can make geometric and deliberate patterns, or we can experiment with freely discovered effects. But although a single decorated shape hung from a thread makes a mobile, like the square it is only a beginning. We can learn if we are prepared to experiment and to look at the way one discovery can lead on to the next.

If we can hang one shape so that it moves, we can hang any number of shapes, and in various different ways. The round shapes in Fig. 24 are suspended so that they will have maximum movement. In order to get this, when two or more shapes are put together, the thread between the shapes must be tied off at the fixture points and cut (Fig. 25). It must not be continued from one shape across the next and up to the top.

This is a small point but it is important if we are to get maximum movement into our mobiles. If the two shapes are strung together as shown, a separate movement will be possible in both of them; one can go one way, and one the other. This is not as critical in a simple two-shape mobile as it might be in some of our later work with more shapes. But if we learn techniques in the early stages they will help us in later works when we are concentrating on more creative discoveries.

Fig. 24 Shapes can be combined and hung.

At this point we can also consider the order in which shapes in a mobile are best strung. This process is always easiest when the stringing is done from the bottom upwards. The order of tying in the example illustrated is indicated by the numbers. A point of balance must be found at the top of the lower shape (1) (Fig. 25), and the thread tied. This can then be cut as a short length and tied at the the lower point of the upper shape (2). The final point of balance at the top of the upper shape (3) can finally be tied off with the hanging thread.

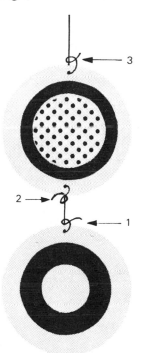

Fig. 25 Movement is less restricted when hung shapes are tied off separately.

In the illustration of the two shapes hung together as a simple mobile, the decoration on the shapes is kept deliberately simple. This is a quality to be aimed for in mobiles. Decoration, no matter how it is applied, should be as simple and immediate as possible, because the mobile must inevitably be seen from some distance away, and also because it will be moving. Clutter and fussy details which must be looked at closely will be out of place on mobiles, and also in much of our later work with paper.

When we set out to cut and hang shapes, we can bear in mind that we will be hanging them from one point. The circles in the mobile illustrated will not, of course, change if the hanging point is varied around the outer edge. But other shapes will change, and we will have to make decisions about where we are going to put the holes for the threads.

We can see this illustrated in Fig. 26. Each pair of triangles is exactly the same, but none of the hanging combinations is identical, and there are other arrangements possible. This sort of changing potential will occur when we make mobiles of anything but round shapes. It is a point we can consider when we make decisions about shapes and how we will hang them.

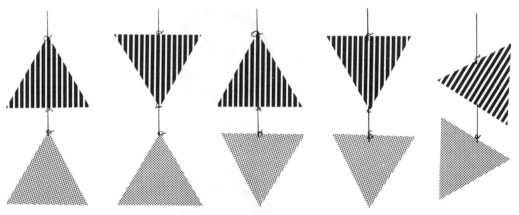

Fig. 26 Hung shapes can be joined in many different ways.

Mirror Mobiles or Reflections

The Mirror Mobile or Reflection is a simple fun exercise in which we can use some of our everyday experience of people, and some of the shape experience we have gained from earlier exercises.

For this exercise the shapes must be cut twice, each of them possibly a little larger than this page, although anyone who wants to work smaller is of course entitled to do so. In some cases the size of the work will be dictated by the material used. A thick paper or thin card would make the best starting point for the Mirror Mobile. In the example shown (Fig. 27) the shapes will be familiar or recognizable to those of us who have been involved in some of the earlier exercises.

Fig. 27 Mirror Mobiles or Reflections.

When we have cut the two background shapes for the Mirror Mobiles, we can develop them with features cut from scraps of paper. Again these should be kept simple. When we work with paper we are not trying to create like-nesses of things and people, or to make real portraits. In paper play a nose can be a triangle, and a circle with a dot can be an eye.

We can leave out features when they are not essential. If there is a moustache shape applied, the mouth can be taken for granted. Or it can be entirely left out, as in the smaller and sad faces. The simpler we can make the statement in paper the more fun it is likely to be. But simplicity is something we have to work for. It is usually better to keep our scissor cuts direct and clean when we work with paper, and it is often better to leave things out entirely, rather than to struggle with complex problems of shape and detail. In many instances these will in any case probably not be possible with a simple material like paper.

With the Mirror Mobiles we can concentrate on finding simple face shapes, like the ones around us: long thin ones, fat ones, squarish ones, hairless ones. A few Mirror Mobiles made in bright colours can make an interesting party decoration. Or they could liven up a classroom. They could be of all the people in the class, although they must suggest identities rather than make accurate portraits. When there are twenty or thirty Mirror Mobiles hanging in one room, and when they all move slightly in the breeze, the effect can be quite amusing.

For large areas, like halls or classrooms where it is difficult to stick or pin threads to the ceiling, a few strings stretched across the room will make it possible to hang the mobiles.

Mirror Mobiles or Reflections might be fun in the classroom, or a few of them in the home might make friends and relations look to see if they are perhaps included. If we make some of them we might look a little more closely at our own reflections when they occur in water or on polished surfaces. We do after all see our own reflections every day of our lives—although not perhaps in quite the same way as the hanging shapes in Mirror Mobiles.

Multiple Mobiles

When we hang two shapes in a vertical arrangement we get a pattern of movement. If we can hang two shapes we can hang any number of shapes in order to get a variety of exciting and different movements. But it is once again useful for us to start with familiar shapes and to consider some of the ways in which a larger number of shapes can be put together.

In Fig. 28 the shapes are again familiar and it should not be difficult for any one of us to understand how they have

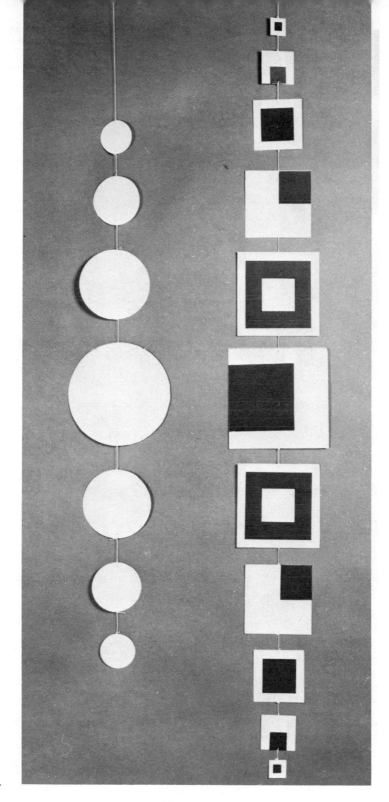

Fig. 28 Vertical mobiles
can have a deliberately
organized development.

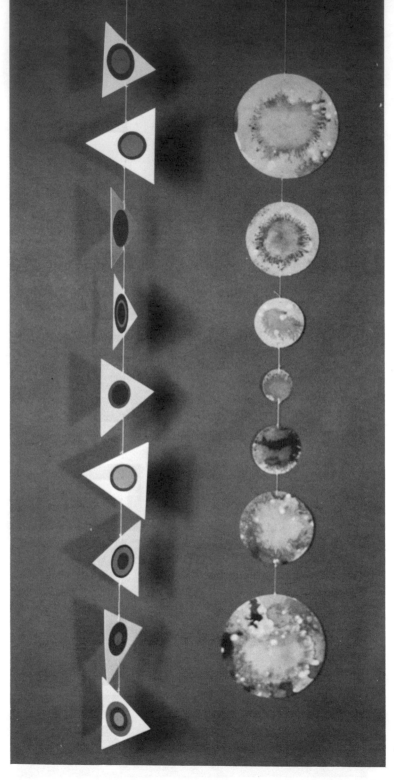

Fig. 29 Surface treatment
can be precise or free.

been arranged. In both examples the shapes grow larger
from the top to the centre, and then decrease in the same
way to the bottom. There is nothing special about this
arrangement. It merely illustrates a type of mobile in
which there is deliberate organization rather than haphazard effect. In some cases the accidental effect of chance
shapes and arrangements might turn out to be visually very
exciting, but our concern at the moment is with simple
ways in which we can control and handle the material.

In Fig. 28 the development of shapes, hung in a vertical
arrangement from small to large and back again to small, is
further exploited in the squares by the addition of other
squares. These have been cut and added before the shapes
were strung together. It is usually best for any surface
treatment to be completed before the shapes of a mobile
are strung together. At this stage, and in more complex
hanging arrangements, any sticking and painting should be
done before the stringing is started. The stringing is a
clean and final operation which will add new life to our
shapes, and it is a pity to ruin it with dirty finger marks.

The movement of the shapes shown in these examples
has been deliberately stopped, but in the triangular mobile
(Fig. 29), which relates to a problem considered previously
in Fig. 26, the movement factor is retained and we find new
shapes emerging in a number of different ways: in the
triangles themselves, in their applied circles and in the cast
shadows which can be seen on the background.

We can also notice in this example that, because it is a
multiple arrangement of shapes, the distance between them
has been kept as short as possible. This is obviously
necessary in multiple arrangements since they should be
able to hang freely wherever they are finally placed. In any
room or classroom, mobiles which are hanging too low
will be quickly knocked about and damaged.

In the second example illustrated (Fig. 29), an arrangement of circles reverses the pattern development of the
circles in the previous illustration. There is also a quite
different sort of decoration applied. The circles have in
this case been freely treated with wet colour in order to
make an overall visual effect. Before the circles were cut
the card was made wet and coloured inks were dripped
onto the wet surface. To avoid unnecessary waste the ink
was taken from the bottle with drinking straws used as
simple pipettes, so that the drops falling on the wet

surface could be controlled. The card was dried, and since it was to be used in a mobile it was treated in the same way again on the reverse side. When it was finally dry it was pressed flat so that the circles could be cut accurately. The cut parts of the decorated cards were kept for use in later work.

There are, as we know, many different ways in which these surfaces could have been treated. In this case ink was used. This was dripped onto the surface, but it could equally as well have been applied with a pen or a brush, or with a piece of wood with the end cut to a suitable shape. It could also have been applied with a piece of rolled paper or a piece of cut card, or with a piece of string with the ends frayed.

The inks could have been used by themselves or they could have been combined with other colours. We are learning as we go on to control and exploit our paper, and we should be beginning to see that, although this is a simple material, it has vast potential. When we have cut shapes we can paint, print, soak, scratch or investigate any other sort of surface treatment. Sometimes if we experiment we will make a mess, but this should lead us to new experiment. There is scope for as much of this as we are prepared to undertake.

Mobiles of shapes suspended vertically one above the other can be made in many different shapes. In Fig. 22 we saw how various treatments of basic shapes would give us new shapes to play with, like the plain shapes in Fig. 30. This shape has been developed from a simple treatment of rectangles, and the more complex shapes in the one next to it from the exploration of rectangles and circles. The surface treatment of the more complex shapes combines the use of paint and of shapes cut from packaging and wrapping papers.

Reference has already been made to the use of printed wrapping papers as a source of decoration, and when we have used some of it in a number of the exercises we might begin to see that it would take a great deal of both time and skill to make the effect freehand. By now we should be collecting as much brightly coloured packaging material as we can get our hands on, and we should be storing it away, preferably neat and flat in a folder for future use.

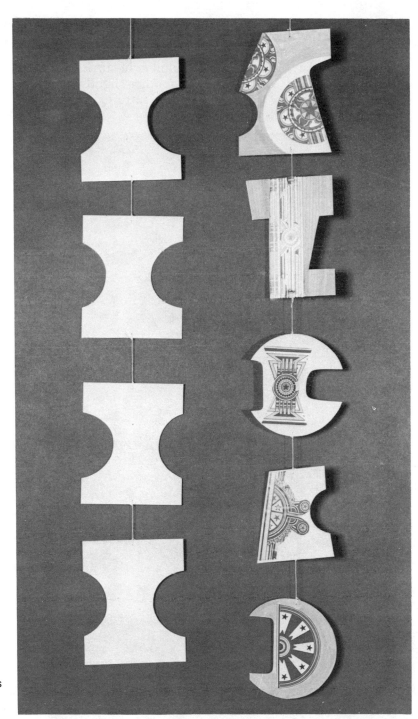

Fig. 30 New shapes can be discovered by experiment.

It is often a mistake in craftwork to get too serious about our ability and the things we make. We were introduced to Mirror Mobiles previously as a fun exercise and now, having looked at the potential of a number of shapes hung together vertically, we can attempt another slightly light-hearted variation of the idea. We can introduce simple faces into our mobiles.

**Mobiles
With Faces**

Fig. 31 Faces can be added—at the top . . .

Fig. 32 . . . or at any other point.

Vertical mobiles made up of a number of shapes with applied pattern can have faces added to make them into fun decorations (Fig. 31). As we saw before, the faces can be as simple as we like to make them. In the first example the face is merely suggested with a triangle and circles on a square. These shapes, including the darker circles in the eyes, are cut out rather than painted to retain the simple precise treatment used in the other shapes.

To be slightly more enigmatic, a long mobile with a face included does not have to have the face at the top. Features can be made on any one of the shapes. We can please ourselves where we put them (Fig. 32). We do not have to ask anyone, nor do we have to keep to any set rules. If we want to play with any number of shapes hung in a straight line, we can do what we like to make them into attractive and colourful decorations. And if we want to include faces for fun, we can do so—where and how we like. We are now able to use the techniques we have learned so that we can play with paper in a variety of new ways.

It might be interesting to see how our friends respond to Mobiles With Faces. We can hang some of the ones we make in our homes or at school, or we might fold them and send them through the post as greetings cards—or even as gifts for special occasions. It is possible now to buy mobiles in various shapes. These are usually in card because, as we have, the manufacturers have seen that it is a light material. And there must be many houses which now have a mobile hung somewhere. If we make them with some care, and if we can keep them crisp and clean, our own Mobiles With Faces should make acceptable presents to many of our friends.

Horizontal Developments

When we have looked a little at the potential of shapes hung vertically we can develop our work into arrangements in which the shapes are hung together so that they spread sideways or horizontally.

In Fig. 33 the squares which were used in the vertical hanging in Fig. 28 are organized into a different arrangement. In this case the large square, formerly at the centre, is used as a hanger for the other shapes.

Fig. 33 Mobiles can be developed in horizontal arrangements.

48 We can see how this sort of arrangement works by considering the simpler example next to it. In this case the lower two squares are suspended separately from the bottom edge of the upper square. The important thing to see is that, although the squares will move independently, they are so arranged that they will not touch at any point during the movement. The two squares overlap at the middle, but one has been tied sufficiently low beneath the other to allow them to move at all times in their own hanging space.

In the same way in the more complex example each of the squares has its own territory, and although they can all move separately in their own directions, no one shape will inhibit the movement of any other.

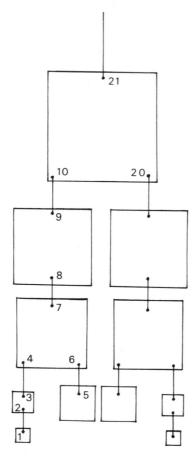

Fig. 34 Hanging sequence from bottom to top.

To make this sort of arrangement of any number of
shapes it is again necessary to start at the bottom and to
work progressively upwards to the top. A suitable hanging
sequence is demonstrated in the diagram Fig. 34. If one of
the smallest shapes is tied first at its point of balance [1],
the tying sequence can be continued to make a complete
unit on the left side for fixing to the top shape [10]. A
similar sequence can be followed with the unit on the right
which can also be finally tied to the top shape [20]. When
both the units are attached to the top square a final point of
balance can be found so that the mobile can be hung from
the top thread [21].

The point of balance in this example is predictably in
the centre because the shapes and their arrangement are
symmetrical throughout. On other occasions it might be
necessary to search for the point of balance by using a trial
and error method with a spike or with a needle. The best
sort of spike is the bradawl which is a tool with a handle. If
small holes are made at the top of any shape where the
point of balance seems to be likely, the tool can be moved
from side to side until the mobile hangs correctly on it.

In this example of a horizontal arrangement one of the
component units, the top square, is used as a support or
hanger for the other shapes. It is possible to do this whenever one of the shapes is large and adequately strong to
support the rest, but sometimes it will be necessary to use a
hanging bar as a support.

In the two examples in Fig. 35 short lengths of wire are
used as supports for the shapes. Either wire or thin strips of
cane or wood can be used in the construction of mobiles.
In this instance the wire has been bent with pliers at the
ends, and has also been bent slightly at the point of
balance.

It is useful when tying mobiles on wire supports to
cement the knots when they are finally placed with blobs
of transparent glue which will harden and keep them
permanently in position. If wood is used it will be enough
to cut small grooves at the fixture points so that the thread
can be tied tightly and without any risk of it slipping off
balance.

In the paired circles in Fig. 35 the blobs of glue have
been applied carefully so that there is no obvious mess. In
all craftwork, even at the most simple level, we can be careful
in the way we use adhesives. It is not necessary to plaster

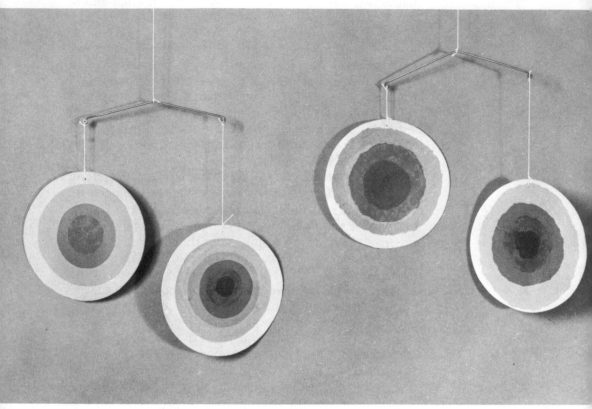

Fig. 35 A hanging bar may be introduced as a support.

glues all over any fixtures. Over-glueing is expensive and messy, and it is not possible to work well with fingers which are crusted with layers of hardening glue. The impact adhesives available today are usually very efficient if the makers' instructions are followed. It helps when working to have a few scraps of card, about the size of one's palm, and some simple card shapes which can be used as spatulas. A little glue squeezed onto a piece of the card can be applied where required with the spatula. This will avoid squeezing too much glue onto the work, and the card and spatula can be thrown away at the end of a working session.

The shapes in Fig. 35 also illustrate the different use of edge treatment in applied decoration. In the example on the left, tissue paper shapes have been cut with scissors and stuck on. But on the right, they have been torn free-hand, giving a much softer edge although they are less precise as shapes. The different visual effects of torn or cut papers, are small points which we might consider in our work, especially when we use papers for the surface treatment of some of the things we will make.

A method of finding the point of balance between separately hung shapes, is illustrated in Fig. 36. This is a trial and error method, in which a knife blade is used under the supporting wire. The knife must be held very still, and the wire from which the shapes are hanging, must be

Fig. 36 The point of balance can be found by trial and error.

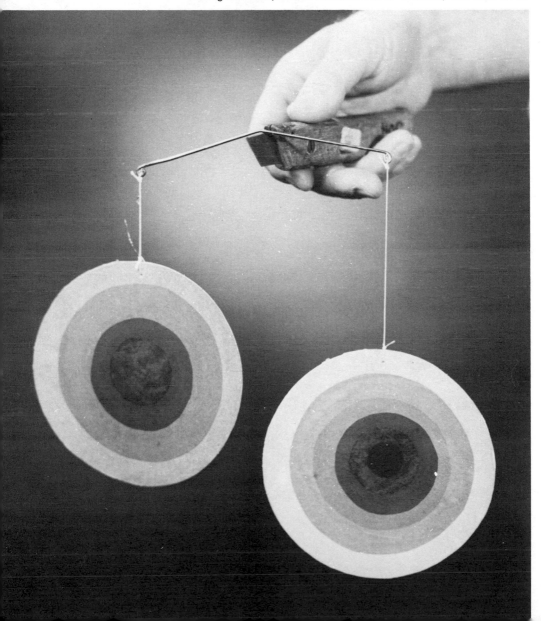

Fig. 37 Shapes can make units for further balancing.

moved carefully across the edge until it can be made to balance. When the point of balance has been established, the wire can be bent slightly downwards as shown. The thread for hanging the shapes can then be tied and fixed with a blob of glue. If a wooden support is used, the knife blade can be eased gently into the wood at the point of balance, and a shallow v-shaped cut can be made for the thread.

Two shapes like those illustrated can be combined with other shapes by the addition of more supporting bars as in Fig. 37. In this case the first two units have been assembled separately and then fixed to the top support so that they cannot touch. This has finally been balanced and tied so that all the shapes can move independently, making an interesting pattern of movement and a possibly more interesting pattern of cast shadows.

The next few illustrations are for anyone who wants to go on to more complex mobiles. There are some of us, who will get a quiet pleasure from the experience of cutting and balancing shapes in complex arrangements, but for others this could be a tedious chore. We are all different in some way.

For those who cannot be bothered with more complicated mobiles, it might be best to jump from here to Fig. 44. There is no point in making our work tiresome. For those who are intrigued by the effect of balance and movement, the examples illustrated from Figs. 38 to 43 offer the prospect of a different type of arrangement in each case.

In Fig. 38 the four shape combination seen in the previous illustration is used as one unit balanced against a unit of two shapes on the other side. We can see from this a simple point of technique in mobile construction. As each new unit is added to an arrangement a new supporting bar must be introduced, and although the arrangement will grow sideways it will also grow upwards at the same time. Using this as a principle, it is theoretically possible to combine as many shapes as we like into a mobile. The six shapes shown in Fig. 38 and suspended finally from the top thread, could themselves become a unit of a much larger mobile. To make this effectively it would perhaps be best for a group of people to work together. It might be an exercise for a class or for a club, or even perhaps for a few friends working together.

54

Fig. 38 Units can grow.

For the even more ambitious, and some of us might come back to this after gaining more skill from working in other parts of the book, there are other quite different possibilities in the arrangement of mobiles.

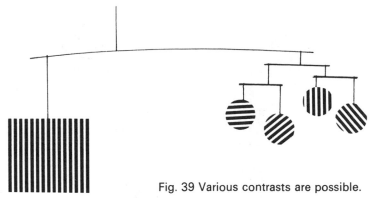

Fig. 39 Various contrasts are possible.

In Fig. 39 a unit of four small shapes is suggested balanced against a single larger shape. If we now work in this sort of way we can introduce a new element into our work. Instead of just having the moving shapes we can also make contrasts between them.

In Fig. 40 the contrast is even more obvious, with the three larger shapes moving round the solitary smaller one. The shapes and decoration in these examples are selected for convenience, and are of course only some of the very many possible alternatives. In this sort of arrangement, or in any sort with such pronounced contrast between the units, we must expect to find the point of balance offset from the centre, and much closer to the heavier part of the arrangement.

Fig. 40 The point of balance will not always be central.

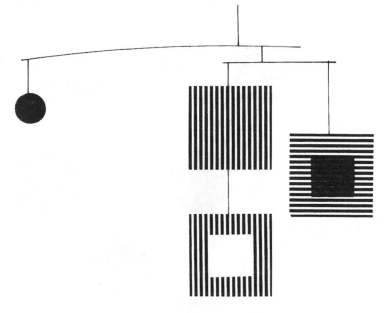

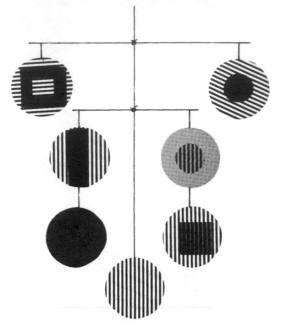

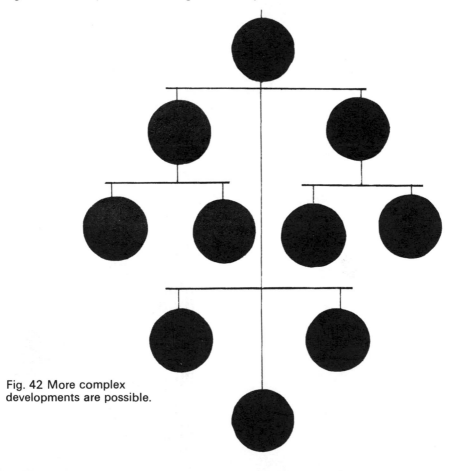

Fig. 41 Various symmetrical arrangements are possible.

Fig. 42 More complex
developments are possible.

In the symmetrical arrangement in Fig. 41 there are three separate units intended to move on a central axis. In this case it would be best to tie off each unit separately at the supporting bars, the single shape at the bottom being tied first at the lower one, which can then be tied to the one above it before the thread is extended at the top. In this sort of arrangement, which can go on growing upwards and outwards, the shapes can be packed in a close cluster. It is also possible after starting like this to make a development back to the centre again as in Fig. 42, but the top shape in this case would have to be cut from a card strong enough to support the rest of the mobile.

In Fig. 43 both vertical and horizontal growths are included. The three shapes strung together on the right could be extended to any number, and the lower shapes on the left could carry their own shapes on horizontal supports. There are many different combinations possible.

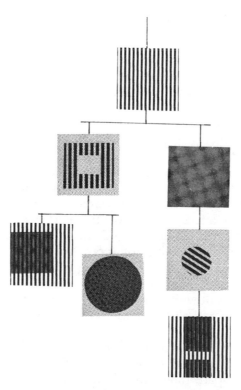

Fig. 43 Similar shapes can be grouped differently.

Mobiles of any shapes made like these more complex examples are, of course, only possible where there is patient interest and an adequate supporting skill. The shapes are not difficult to cut or decorate, and as we will see in later examples, all sorts of shapes can be hung. But the process of balancing complex shapes takes time, and is best attempted where there is both space and quiet. These are both desirable aspects of any craft situation, but where it is not possible for them to exist adequately there are still plenty of fun opportunities which can be attempted in even the most crowded of rooms.

Face Mobiles

When we worked with shapes before, we put faces on them to make simple fun decorations. Now we can make faces deliberately and hang them. We have new and interesting shapes to use. Using a suitably thin card we can make face mobiles in any of the arrangements suggested in previous exercises.

We can make the mobile up with a few faces as in Fig. 44, or if we have adequate technical skill we can have a whole crowd of faces. Face mobiles always seem to work. This is perhaps because we are used to being surrounded by moving faces at some time. We will all have been in a crowd, or in a 'sea' of faces, and we perhaps tend to look at faces at such times, rather than at people as whole persons.

The shapes in Fig. 44 are not the usual shapes we find as faces, but this is now a familiar shape to us and it is interesting to see how the addition of simple eyes and a nose will again transform a shape and give it character. We can use any shape to make a face. We can try this perhaps on scraps of paper and card scattered round the workroom. It is interesting to make a collage of scrap faces, using scraps of all shapes and sizes. It is interesting because we will find that, no matter how extravagantly shaped the faces are, the end result will still look like a crowd of people. Perhaps we should all look closer at the shapes of our own faces.

A spare wall in a room, or in a classroom, is an ideal opportunity for a scrap crowd of home-made faces. The project could fill in spare moments of time over a long period, and might keep us interested on all those odd occasions when we have almost nothing to do.

Fig. 44 Face Mobiles can be the beginning of a moving crowd.

Mobile Faces which can be made in any shapes and in arrangements of any numbers must, like all mobiles, be decorated on both sides. But again they need not be the same on both sides. A mobile of hanging faces could be awake on one side and asleep on the other (Fig. 45), which to some people might account for the startled expressions on the awake side. They could be red on one side and healthy, and pale on the other. On one side they could all have open mouths like a choir, or they could all be wearing sunglasses like people on a beach. If we really look at people we will find ideas of our own which we might try, like some of the shapes which follow.

Fig. 45 They can be different on the reverse side.

When we find different shapes and make them into Mobile Faces they can be very amusing and we are working, light-heartedly, as we should with this material. But the shapes we make can suggest new ideas. The shapes in the previous exercise, with the cut-out pieces at the sides, might invite the addition of new moving shapes.

Ear-ring Faces

Ear-ring Faces (Fig. 46) are mobiles of such shapes with new additions. The additions will again move independently and add to the fun of the hung shapes. The ear-rings can be simple shapes with pattern, and they can be hung singly or, if there is room as in the longer example, as combined units. In this case the earlier experiments we did with simple shapes hung vertically are applied in an actual making situation, and the technique helps us with our work—if Ear-ring Mobiles can be called work.

A touch of silver or gold card, or even of aluminium cooking foil, on the ear-rings will cause them to reflect light as they move and will add to the effect.

Fig. 46 Ear-ring Faces.

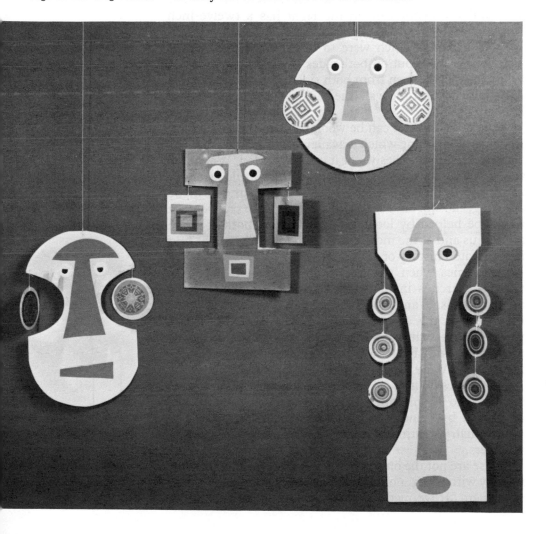

When we are working with paper or card there is no reason why we should not include other materials, particularly materials which are both easy to get and easy to use—like the string on the Hair Faces in Fig. 47. This is ordinary coarse parcel string which has been dyed in cold water dyes and dried before use. The sort of ordinary cold water dyes which can be bought in many hardware stores is suitable, and it is not necessary to fix the colour since the string is unlikely ever to be washed.

In the examples illustrated, simple and slightly developed shapes have been used. For this exercise the hair was measured in lengths. The lady on the left has 1-metre hair, and the gentleman on the right has a twelve-inch moustache!

In Hair Faces which were to be free hanging, a face would have to be put on both sides of the shape, but one lot of hair will be seen from both sides. If they were made to be hung against the wall, the back of the shape could be left quite plain.

The string hair—it can be wool, rope, rag, paper, wood shavings or anything which is available—can be fixed to the faces with impact adhesive, or it can be stapled. When it is added it provides new opportunities for simple arrangement and decoration. Hair Faces, although they can be amusing, can still have style. If we are going to try them we might be helped by looking at hair styles, both at those around us and at the more extravagant ones we might find in illustrated history or geography books.

Sometimes when we are at school we will be doing various exercises in measuring. It is necessary to learn about dimension and area. But when we have measured all the parts of the school we can reach—and the school playground—we might persuade someone to let us do some more work with Hair Faces used as exercises in accurate measuring. Many of us learn best when we are playing.

Hair Faces do not, of course, have to be human; nor do they have to be only single hangers like those shown. They can begin by being of anything which can reasonably be given a hairy treatment: a lion with a mane, or a cat with whiskers.

These are not the only examples of faces we can make as we play with paper, nor is hanging the only thing we can do with them. If we made Hair Faces like those illustrated,

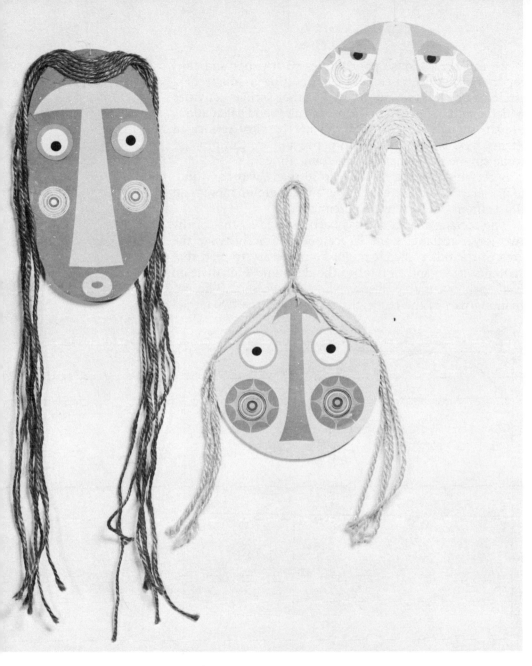

63

Fig. 47 Hair Faces.

and if we put a flap on the back of each one in the form of a horizontal strip of paper fixed at both ends, we could slip them on our hands and use them as puppets. Faces in paper can be made as various puppets, or they can be made as a variety of masks.

If we can use various opportunities with paper and card for measuring exercises, and even cutting a square or a circle can be this, we can try many other similar activities which might involve us in the use of rulers and calculations —even though the exercises will not be very serious in themselves. We can play with paper and we can practise some simple mathematics at the same time.

A rectangle can be divided up in many ways and into many shapes, and the next few examples are no more than illustrations of a very wide potential.

The rectangle (Fig. 48) has been divided so that of the two lower rectangles the larger one is exactly twice the area of the other one. It might be necessary to read that sentence again and to refer to the diagram. This division has been accurately measured—not guessed. The remaining part of the rectangle, from which the two circles

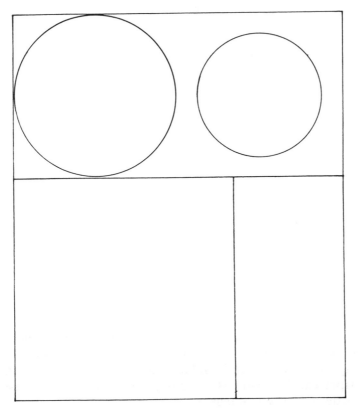

Fig. 48 Division of rectangle for Area Hangers.

have been cut need not be of any specified dimension, but
in the exercise as shown, one of the circles has been made
as large as is possible in this rectangle.

In Fig. 49 these shapes have been made up into two
mobiles of two units each—a fat man and his wife; and we
know that the area of his body shape is twice that of hers.
We can demonstrate it by decorating the shapes with
equal-size squares as shown. The man and wife, hung
together in close attachment on a horizontal support
(Fig. 35) would make an interesting end product after
several processes of accurate measuring and cutting.

Fig. 49 Man and Wife Area Hangers.

Fig. 50 Number Hangers.

As an exercise this is not as tiresome as some types of measuring and calculating might be. We need to be able to measure and we need to know about area; and usually the more exercises we do, the more we are likely to improve in ability. A family of figures with their bodies measured and coloured in brightly contrasting squares could really get us working with our rulers—and with our hands and minds. And the results could be much more exciting visually than squares and other shapes drawn in exercise books.

There are also some of us who like to work precisely, and who get satisfaction from accuracy and from well ordered processes.

In Fig. 50 there is a variation on the fat man idea. In this illustration the Area Hanger has a body made from a rectangle which has certain proportions. This is the Twelve by Two Hanger, which might be labelled on the back: $12 \times 2 = ?$. Most of us will know the answer but others will still have to learn it. There is a whole family waiting to be made to go with this Hanger. And there are other families beside this one. We could also make this one, or one of equivalent size and area, in other ways. How many other ways are there of making it?

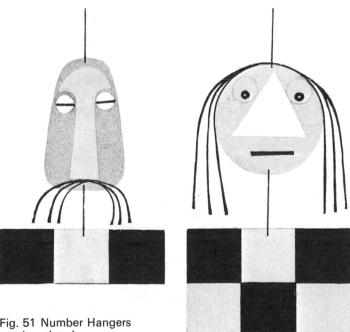

Fig. 51 Number Hangers
can be related . . .

Fig. 52...from one to the next and so on.

If we can play with this Hanger, and if we can write in clear bold numbers a correct statement on the back of it, there are other statements we might write on the backs of the three Hangers in Figs. 51 and 52. In these illustrations Hair Faces from the previous exercise have been combined with Area Hangers. As the bodies increase in size, the length of hair also increases. The faces change in shape but this is a matter of choice. The progression we see is a number progression in which the height of the rectangle (or body) changes from one shape to the next. These, and the rest of the family if we like to make them, can be suspended from a string and hung in a line for future reference. With an exercise like this we might be learning as we play, and we can also make our surroundings not only attractive but sometimes also useful and informative.

The squares in Number Hangers, which should be reasonably accurate, can be made, either by cutting and sticking paper squares on a background—in which case a pencil grid could be drawn first, or by the use of a ruler and felt-tip. If bold and accurate lines are made with these, the correct squares can be filled in afterwards. It helps, if we are concentrating hard, to mark the squares to be filled in before we work, so that we can never accidentally fill in one of the plain ones.

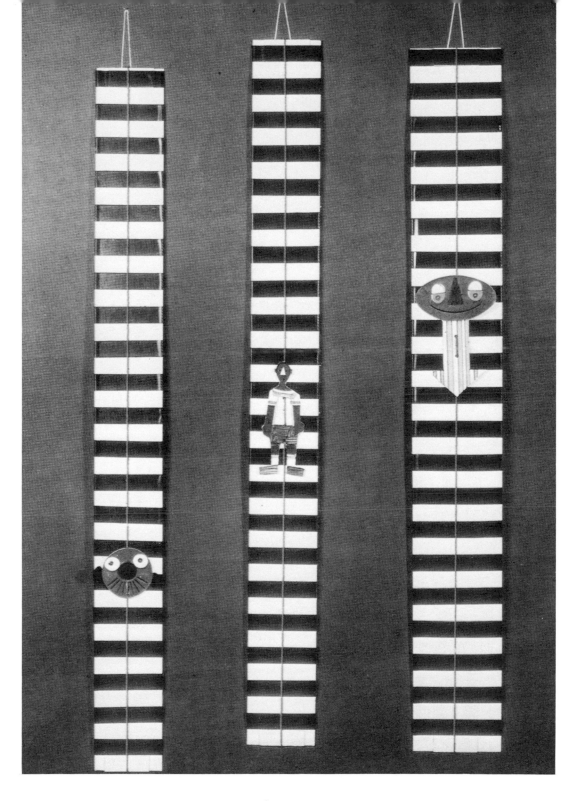

Scorers.

Scorers   Most of us have a favourite team we support, and having
worked accurately on strips of card, we might like to extend
the exercise into another play opportunity. We might like
to record our team's score as the season progresses, or
some of us might have other opportunities to check off a
series of numbers. We might be keeping a check on money
saved towards a target figure, or we might be ticking off the
days to the holidays.

To help us keep a record of these, or any other similar
things we are involved in, we can make scoring devices
with strips of white card measured and marked off in
equal sections (see opposite page 68). These marked cards
can be fitted with a single string along the length, and the
ends of the string can be fixed out of sight at the back
with adhesive tape.

A movable pointer or indicator can be fitted to the
Scorer so that it can be adjusted up or down the string to
mark off any number of divisions. If the movable part is
made with card and is pierced with two holes it can be
fitted to the string as shown in Fig. 53. The string must
come from the back of the pointer through one hole and
must be threaded back through the other. When it is
strung in this way, with the string taut across the Scorer,
the pointer will stay in place at any point.

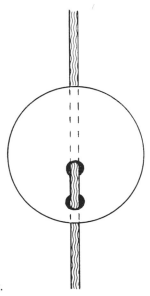

Fig. 53 Movable pointer for the Scorer.

The pointer can be any shape. It can be a simple arrow. Or it can be a face or a figure. One sometimes sees this sort of scorer on a larger scale outside hospitals or churches where there is an appeal for funds taking place. It is a form of graph, or a method of recording amounts. For our purposes the Scorers can have light-hearted pointers which can be moved to record goals, cash amounts, days, house points at school—or anything which provokes enough interest in us to want to go to the trouble of making them.

An alternative method to the one in which string is used is illustrated in Fig. 54. In this type of Scorer the pointer itself is more dominant than the marked off strip. Any shape could be decided on for the pointer but it should prefer-ably be in the form of a face—animal or human; we can play as we like. To make the up and down movement possible, two parallel cuts *A* and *B* must be made in the middle of the pointer, like those at the top and bottom of the clown's mouth.

The marked strip must be slightly less wide than these cuts so that it can be threaded through them. Like the string in the previous exercise the strip must be threaded

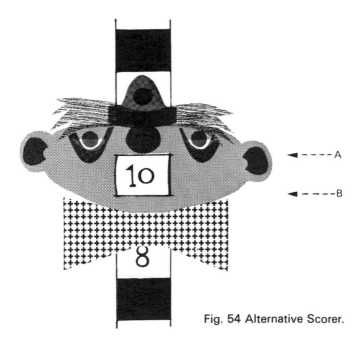

Fig. 54 Alternative Scorer.

through from the back to the front, and then back through the other cut. The part of the strip appearing at the mouth of the pointer can record the current score. For this purpose numbers can be marked on the white parts of the movable strip.

If space is limited for the Scorers they can be hung sideways, and the pointers designed to mark off the score by moving from left to right. Photographs of favourite teams or of individual players can be included in the design of the Scorers—perhaps at the end of the marked strip.

This is a way of playing with our materials in order to record someone else's play. As an aid to construction we might use black adhesive tape to mark the gradations. This is available in rolls in various makes, and is usually of suitable width. If it is cut and applied carefully it will save a lot of time with pen or brush and will probably result in a neater end product.

If they are put away carefully and looked after, Scorers can be used for a number of seasons. It is not necessary to be over fussy about hoarding our work; there are many other things for us to make yet. But this item is one we might be glad to use over and over again. Scorers might therefore be made perhaps with extra special care.

Various Hangers

Before we consider developing our work into the exploration of new forms we might try some other opportunities for hanging shapes. So far we have concentrated on human shapes when we have moved away from merely decorative shapes and have introduced a recognizable identity into our work. There are lots of other opportunities for play and experiment with mobiles.

Fig. 55 Simple shapes will work differently.

In an earlier exercise when we cut a circle we saw that this could be made to suggest a simple human face by the addition of a triangle and two circles. If we now change the arrangement of these shapes we can get a different identity. The shapes in Fig. 55 are basic and familiar, but the change through deliberately different arrangement opens new possibilities. To see the change effectively it might be necessary for some of us to isolate the bird or the human by covering one of them with a hand.

Bird Mobiles

In a previous exercise we hung a number of circles on a single vertical and considered the potential of their movement. In a subsequent exercise we made them into decorative hangers with faces included. The circles strung together in Fig. 56 would not be convincing to an ornithologist, but they could be patterned in any number of different ways and illustrate a simple development of the last shape in the previous illustration. The circles and triangle can be variously placed on the background to suggest hanging birds.

It is reasonable, as we develop the opportunities we have for making mobiles, to hang shapes which suggest anything which is not normally firmly anchored to the ground. It would hardly be reasonable to make and hang a series of essentially earthbound objects like gas-stoves or refrigerators, but anything which moves—and certainly anything which is sometimes airborne—can be tried as a mobile.

Birds in variously constructed shapes are obviously very suitable for hanging, and the unhurried movement of some mobiles is very characteristic of some forms of flight. But if we think of birds as suitable shapes for hanging we might have fun if we experiment and play with new ways of making the shapes.

The birds in Fig. 56 are so simple that they merely provide an opportunity for pattern treatments, but there is more potential in the subject. We can play, as we have seen, with the shapes. We can, for example, break them down to new shapes which can be strung together in different ways.

The shapes in Fig. 57 would almost certainly be recognized as birds, but they are really simple and bold shapes abstracted from the original and strung together to allow varied and interesting movements.

Fig. 56 Shapes can be applied in various positions.

Fig. 57 Subjects can be separated into moving parts.

If we can begin to work in this slightly more varied way, we will find ourselves helped if we actually take the trouble to look at the things we want to make. If we are basing our work on birds we should look at them whenever possible, and particularly if we are able to visit a zoo where we will find them in unusual and exciting new shapes and patterns. As we look we will feed into ourselves information for future reference, information about patterns and about shapes which we will later find ourselves using in our work. We should find this possible now because we already know quite a lot about shapes, and when we look we will respond to some of the many differences in shapes and patterns which are all around us.

The birds in Fig. 58 are treated differently again. In this case the mobiles are made up of simple component parts,

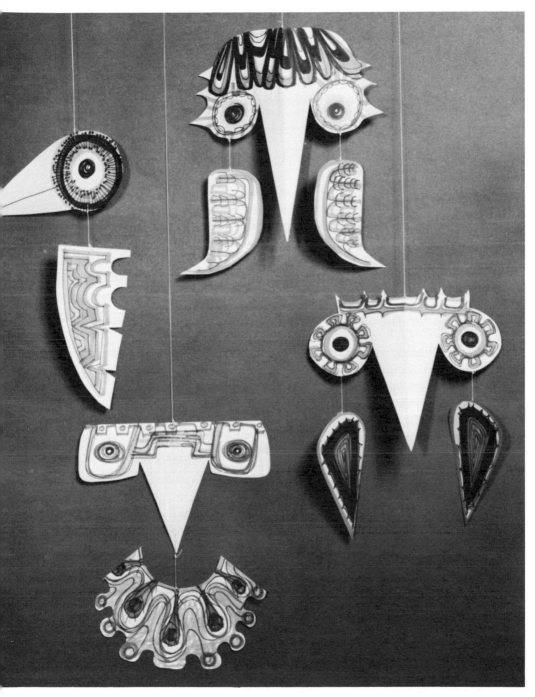

Fig. 58 New ways of treating the subject can be investigated.

but they include in some of the shapes, a decorative treatment of cuts at the edges. This is a technique which we have not yet considered in our work with shapes. We have discovered how to find different shapes, but these have always had unbroken edges. It might be interesting now to consider how many different edge treatments we can cut in a strip of paper. There are of course very many to be discovered, both now and in later exercises. The front-view birds in the illustration also include the use of a centre fold, which allows the cut shape to be made symmetrical, and which allows the form to be kept slightly raised at the front. If the fold is not flattened out completely it can be included as a constructional aid. It strengthens the cut shape, and the contrast on both sides of the fold adds to the visual effect. This is a technique which is considered more fully in later exercises.

Other bird shapes and treatments are possible as mobiles, but the rest can be left to individual experiment. They are waiting to be discovered as we go on to consider other shapes suitable for hanging.

Flowers

When we see flowers they are often moving slightly in a breeze, and they are also very often clustered tightly together. The cluster mobile or close arrangement of shapes which we looked at in earlier exercises is ideal as an exercise which uses flowers as a starting point.

The simple flower shapes in Fig. 59 are hung as a cluster from one larger shape, with care taken to see that they will not touch as they move. In this example the edge cutting suggested in the previous exercise is applied with simple variations. Edge cutting can be worked freely and directly into the material, but in some instances of slightly more complex shapes it might be useful to draw the shapes first, so that they are properly organized round the outer edge.

This is again only one very simple illustration of the many ways there must be of making flowers as flat hanging shapes and, as we have done in the past, we must still be prepared to experiment and explore new possibilities.

The shapes in Fig. 60 retain in some way the quality of flowers but are less usual or commonplace than the more normal shapes made up of petals round a circle. When we are used to cutting paper and experimenting with new shapes we will find ourselves breaking away from conventional or stock images—not necessarily to make better

Fig. 59 Cluster mobiles are suitable for some subjects.

78 things but to extend the scope of our work as we develop confidence and skill. When we look at flowers we see them from many different points of view, and the flowers themselves are very varied in shape. It is again a question of looking to discover. And what we find we can use. Looking is an activity which costs us nothing.

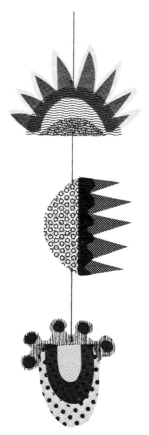

Fig. 60 Familiar subjects can be seen differently.

If we use new flower shapes and patterns in cluster mobiles we might extend the results by including leaf shapes with their own appropriate colours and patterns. Most of us could draw a leaf shape if asked to do so, but here again in our work we will be helped by collecting and looking at actual leaves. They come in many different shapes and sizes, and when we collect and compare them we might find new shapes to cut in paper.

It will sometimes help to make leaf or flower shapes in paper larger than they really are, especially if we intend to use them as decorations. Small shapes can of course be delicate and can make very attractive mobiles for small rooms. But where decorations have to fill large spaces with immediate impact, enlargement and emphasis are necessary processes. The size factor will depend as usual on the material. There is no point in cutting crisp and clean shapes if, when we hang or display them, they flop into misshapen mistakes. We will learn as we work to control the material and to know when we are reaching the size limit with a paper of certain thickness. It is not possible here to state any firm rules about size, since strength and size factors can only be assessed in the actual working situation. If it flops out of shape it is either too big, or the paper is too thin, and we must make our own decisions as we work.

Butterflies and Moths

Like flowers, butterflies or moths are very suitable for flat shape treatment. We can find interesting shapes to cut if we look at book illustrations, or better still at real butterflies or moths. The shapes we must find will be particularly suitable because they are symmetrical and can be cut on a central fold.

If we work from references (Fig. 61) we will find a great deal of subtle variety both in shapes to cut, and in the surface patterns which extend over a wide range of straight and curved lines and shapes. But again it is not necessary to work too closely to reality. It is a matter of looking and selecting and playing with the patterns which appeal to us.

The butterfly shapes in Fig. 62 have been deliberately simplified as a variation on previous exercises with circles. In these instances circles have been cut and then cut again through the diameter to make semi-circles which have then been rearranged on simple body shapes. This is a method of simplification or stylization which can be useful in work with paper, especially when the intention is to make an instant appeal to the eye.

Most of our work in paper will be decorative, and simplification will assist us when we use repetition as a factor. A simplified shape is usually visually suitable for repetition. It is also suitable in a practical sense, in that it can be repeated any number of times with a minimum of

Fig. 61 Symmetrical shapes are easy to cut.

Fig. 62 Simplification is possible.

effort. When this is so, the real creative work can be reserved, after the initial shapes have been decided on, for colour and pattern treatments, which can in any case be demanding enough.

In the Butterfly Mobile (Fig. 62), the shapes are a long way removed from the winged insects known to science, but they are intended to be of general visual appeal, rather than of specialist appeal to the collector. With the shapes simplified it is also possible to simplify the shaping and placing of applied pattern. In the examples shown this relates in some way to the shapes carrying it. The curves and straight edges of these shapes have been incorporated into the patterns deliberately in order to illustrate the scope of the styles and methods open to us. The difference between the two examples, and this is only one of many differences possible, is not a statement of what is right or wrong. It is a statement of opportunity. We must experiment, and we must look and compare. After this we can make and carry out our own decisions.

Balloons

It is hardly necessary to say anything about the way the decorated circles are used in Fig. 63. If we are playing with materials our play will extend over a long period of time. It will not be concentrated into a single process like the examples in this book. As we play from time to time we will explore any opportunity or idea which suggests itself to us. But whenever we get an idea we should either make a note of it for future use, or better still we should work at it straight away.

These balloonists are very simplified people, and they are again far removed from the real thing. But a large hanging shape which is brightly coloured and patterned might lend itself to various interpretations or treatments, like the idea of the balloonists sailing noiselessly through the sky.

The person who really wants to know about ballooning will go to various reference books and to experts or specialists if they are available. He will try to find out as many facts as he can about the sport. But we are less concerned with facts. We know that people sometimes sail through the sky in baskets suspended from large ball shapes. We can accept the activity as a starting point for experiment and play, although there is no reason why this should not lead us to make our own investigations and researches into the history and practice of the sport.

Fig. 63 Many subjects provide play opportunities.

As we play with paper we might well uncover some new area of interest which, as we investigate it, will extend us and make us more interesting as persons. There is much overlap between people and their various interests, and one of the delightful things about the sort of freedom to play which we get from this material is that we can invite ourselves into any activity.

In the illustration shown we can see only one of very many different ways in which we can use man's progress through the sky as a source for our own work. Without taking our feet off the ground even, we could involve ourselves in a form of ballooning, or we could work in many different areas of flight. We could cut and hang paper and card shapes based on any of the exploits of man off the ground, from the earliest mythological adventure of Icarus and Daedalus to the modern successes of the space walkers and astronauts. If we can make a fun version of a balloon with the balloonists we might like to research the real thing. We might refer to earlier ballooning experiments with hot air vehicles which were ornately decorated, or we might look at the strange shapes used in high altitude ballooning. We can make mobiles of parachutists, airships, planes or rockets. There is enough scope for all of us to play with the shapes of flight and space exploration.

Suns

If we are working in any of the opportunities provided by flight and space adventure we might take a light-hearted view of the planets. The moon, sun and stars are simple and attractive shapes for mobiles and decorations, although if we wished to be more accurate we might consider the prospect of other shapes and their movement, like the planets Mercury, Venus, Earth and Mars revolving in a special way round the sun.

The Sun and Moon Mobiles illustrated in Fig. 64 would probably horrify an astronomer. But there are not many of these, and certainly not enough of them to influence our work. The shapes used are again simple and stylized, as are the cut and applied decorations.

We will sometimes, especially in later exercises, want to make simple star shapes. These can be drawn freehand with any number of points, but a simple method for making a six-pointed star is illustrated in Fig. 65. This will be developed later, and it is useful to know that one triangle

Fig. 64 Stars are easy to cut and decorate.

reversed and superimposed on itself will make a symmetrical star shape. There are, of course, other methods of making stars, and we will be involved later in the development of flat shapes to three-dimensional forms. But at this stage the star shown is adequate, and any number of them can be made from one triangle of card, cut and used as a template.

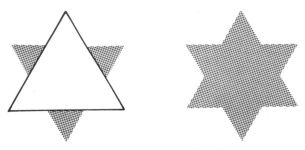

Fig. 65 Method for cutting six-pointed star.

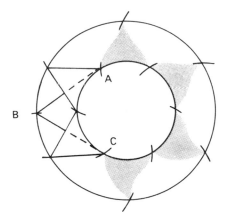

Fig. 66 Method for cutting various suns.

It is also useful to understand how to cut a good symmetrical sun in card. If we start with a circle we can mark the radius of the circle around its circumference as in Fig. 66. We will find if we do this that the radius will mark off as six almost equal divisions.

An inner circle placed somewhere inside the outer one can be marked off with its own radius in the same way, although the starting point should be halfway between two of the points on the outer circumference (Fig. 66*A*).

This is another way of making a six-pointed star, but for our present purpose we are concerned with the sun shape and after marking the circles the points can be joined as shown.

For a sun with twice as many points, like the example illustrated in Fig. 64, the outer circle must be further marked with divisions halfway between those already put in, and the points made as shown (Fig. 66*A–B, B–C*).

Alternative shapes are possible for the points of the sun, like those suggested in the toned areas. For these, or any other alternative shapes, a thin card can be cut to the required shape and used as a template at each point. Suns and any patterns on them should, of course, be very warm in colour and very bright. We can understand, thinking of the sun or looking at it, what sorts of colours we can use, and what is meant when some of them are referred to as warm colours.

Boats   For those who are interested in the sea or are attracted to boats, various projects can be tried in simple boat shapes. A mobile of sailing boats (Fig. 67) would be easy to cut, especially to those of us who like using a ruler and straight lines.

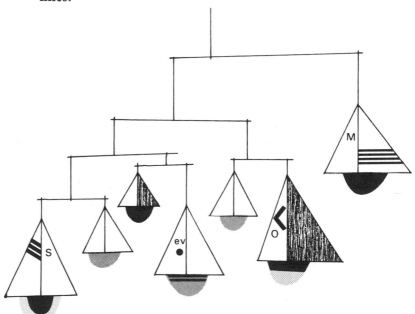

Fig. 67 Boats are suitable subjects for mobiles.

There are certainly many different shapes of yachts and sailing boats, and the ones illustrated are only a pointer to the potential of the subject. But again it will probably be discovered in practice that the reduction of shapes to a simple statement can be visually rewarding in the end product. It is also difficult sometimes to cut intricate details in card. In this case it would probably be technically very difficult to cut masts and lines, and they are best left out. If we worked with a few friends on a boat mobile we might select and include our own special mark and use it with an initial on the sail, in the same way as sailing boats are classified. It would make the units in the mobile specially important to us as we watched the movement. It might even involve us in a simple form of a race. And it would make us think about applied motifs, and then make us look a little more closely at some of the motifs actually used when next we have an opportunity to look at real boats.

If we are considering shapes suitable for hanging exercises we must think about fish. This is, as it should be, a well-known and often used shape for the paper or card mobile. It is right for the subject. When fish are hung up they move and seem to swim. They are easy-to-cut shapes, and they are very suitable for decoration—particularly with stripes and spots. Certainly there is nothing wrong with fish shapes for mobiles, especially if they can be discovered by observation of fish either alive, or perhaps more easily—at the fishmonger's. What we might do, however, is to look for ways of extending the fish as a subject for mobiles.

Fish

We might, for example, hang the fish by the tail or by the mouth—or even upside down as in Fig. 68. We often tend to make things and hang them up in a predictable way. A vertical arrangement of fish all swimming upwards and attached from mouth to tail might be interesting. If we take the trouble to observe some of them closely in a fish tank we will see that they do in fact swim in all directions and not just sideways.

In the examples shown (Fig. 69) other different fish treatments are suggested, although these are slightly more complex than the simple shapes. In this case the fish shapes have been divided into component parts, like the birds in earlier exercises, and then put together in various arrangements. In the lower right-hand example simple

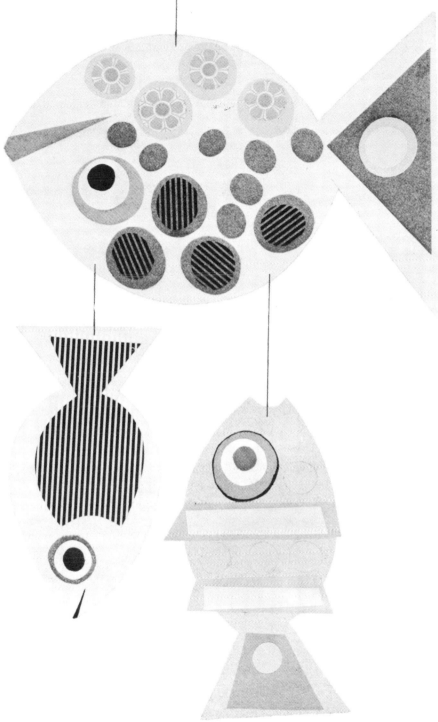

Fig. 68 Familiar shapes can be hung in unexpected ways.

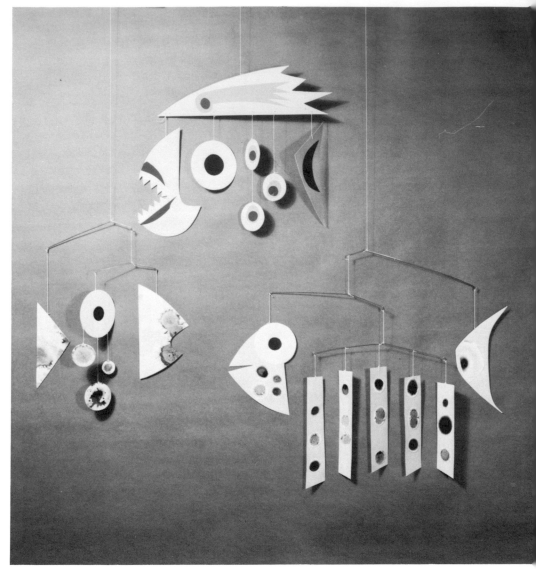

Fig. 69 They can also be cut in separately moving parts.

head and tail shapes are linked together visually with a series of rectangles which suggest the body. The real fish is obviously the tail and the head, and the body could be made up of any shapes.

The other examples are slightly more abstract and perhaps only just recognizable as fish. But, as the word suggests, 'abstraction' is a process which starts with something from which a part is separated. In these examples some of the normal shapes of the fish have been separated and then reassembled, so that they will make patterns of movement as they hang.

The results of these and other similar experiments might sometimes make mobiles which are enigmatic and less than realistic, but if some care is taken with the shapes and if the surface treatments are varied and interesting, the experiments will be original and worth trying. But whatever we do to make something new from a well-known exercise, it will be supported best if we begin by using our eyes to look more closely at the original shape. Fish are varied and interesting and very worth close scrutiny and examination.

Swallowers But to illustrate the point more fully, and before we go on to new experiments, we can consider the fish again as a shape for cutting and hanging. When we look at something we can see it from a number of different viewpoints, although we sometimes tend to forget this. The fish in Fig. 70 are seen directly from the front and are depicted in this way, rather than in the more usual profile or side view (see also opposite page 92).

To make them into a play exercise we might take front shapes and cut large mouths in them so that as they move they can be swallowing other moving shapes. In one of the examples shown one Swallower is swallowing another fish, but in the other example a Swallower is swallowing another Swallower who is swallowing another fish. This is another way we have discovered of making an arrangement of shapes in a mobile—in this case of shapes actually suspended to move inside other shapes.

Swallowers can be of many different shapes and identities. It might be interesting to explore different mouth shapes for them. Frogs, for example, might have semicircular mouths with flat bottoms. It might also be interesting to see how many shapes could be strung together in the act of swallowing before the over-all shape became too big and unwieldy. It requires a little care to match the inside shapes to their openings, and to string them so that they revolve freely. But it is not impossible. And it is interesting.

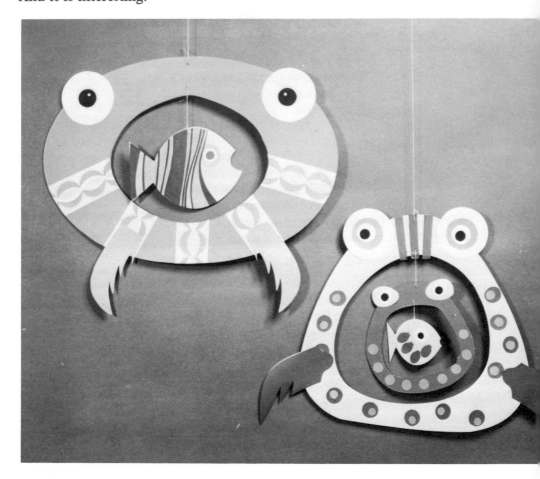

Fig. 70 Swallower swallowing Swallower.

Cats

If we were to draw a cat most of us would probably include a body, a head and a tail. This again makes an opportunity for fun mobiles. We can play with cats in our own way. The body, head and tail, cut separately and strung together will make cats slightly closer perhaps to reality than drawn ones. They will make moving cats! Like the real thing!

Swallower swallowing Swallower.

Fig. 71 Toy cats can move—like the real thing.

The examples shown in Fig. 71 will move slowly, like lazy pets, when they are hung, and they could be further developed in various ways. Instead of having the head at the top, a mobile cat might have it included as a lower shape. If we look closely at the shapes made by cats as they lie about we might find this a reasonable thing to do.

Mobile cats might also be treated like the Hairs (Fig. 47). They could have measured whiskers in string—another measuring exercise; long droopy whiskers or short bristling ones. If everyone in a class made a mobile cat, and if they were all hung in a line side by side on a string stretched across the room, the visual effect would change every time anyone came into the classroom. The cats could be patterned with colours, or they could have many different things used as surface decorations. Spirals of string or wool stuck flat would make them look like curly-haired cats. They could have spots cut from scraps of richly patterned materials, or corrugated card stripes.

These are toy cats, and we are only using the approximate shape of the real things. We can add to them and decorate them as freely as we like, and sometimes the more experimental we make the decoration the more fun we might get from the exercise.

A moving cat, designed small enough to go into an envelope without being folded, could be decorated on one side and could have writing on the other. It would make a letter or an unusual invitation card. It is sometimes difficult to write letters to our friends when they are in hospital. A Hanging Cat letter, or one made up as any other animal, must surely cheer them up when they receive it.

Tails

The cat letter need not hang from a string. If we are really involved in this sort of work we should be beginning to develop variety in it through the imaginative use of our materials. We could still make and send cats to our friends, but this time we could make them as a simple toy which can be played with or which can be fixed to a flat wall.

It is necessary to look quite hard at the illustrations (Figs. 72 and 73). But this should not be unusual to us since this book is very much concerned with the way we look at things. The cats in both illustrations might look the same but there are subtle differences.

Fig. 72 Tails . . .

The bodies of the cats are simple rounded shapes, but they are not hung freely so that they will move round and round from front to back. They are pinned to the wall with a pin through the centre of the body. In this way they can be rotated with a flick of the fingers, like a Catherine-wheel firework.

The interesting thing is that no matter how much the body is spun, whenever it stops, the head and tail will always be in the right position.

Fig. 73 . . . as a play toy.

In Fig. 72 the cat with the striped body has up and down,
or vertical stripes, and his head and tail are at the sides of
the body. In Fig. 73 his stripes are now horizontal, but his
head and tail are still the right way up, although they are
now at the top and the bottom of the body. A similar change
can be seen happening in the illustrations of the fat spotted
cat.

The secret of Tails is that the head and tail are fixed to
the body very loosely with a brass paper fastener on which
they can rotate freely. The brass paper fastener is of the
type which has a flat head, and is pushed through from the
front to the back where the two points can be opened out
flat. If the hole in the head of the cat is at the top, and if it is
made large enough for the head to be spun round freely on
the fastener, it will always come to rest in the right position
when it is spun round. The paper fastener must not, of
course, be pinched tightly when it is opened at the back
otherwise it will hardly be possible to turn the head at all.

This is not a very serious toy, but it is fun to make and
can be more fun if it is fixed to the wall of one's room, or
perhaps even to the door.

To make this or any other Tail we will need a body shape
which is simple; a round shape for the head, with ears
included—this might recall some of the shapes developed
in our earlier exercises with circles—and an ordinary
uncomplicated sort of tail.

After decorating the shapes and adding the features, we
can fix the head towards the side of the body with a paper
fastener. We can decide on the positioning by placing the
body down flat and putting the head on top of it. If we turn
the body carefully, keeping the head in place, we will begin
to see what it might look like and what it might do when
the head is fixed to it. When we are satisfied with the
positioning we can make the fixture. If possible the holes
should be made with a paper punch, but if this is not
available the cards can be pierced with a bradawl and the
hole enlarged with a nail or a screw. When the head and
body are joined they should move freely, and it should be
possible to spin the head. The same process can now be
followed with the tail, but again there should be no tight-
ness or restriction of movement at the fixture.

The rest is simple. If we hold the body and rock it, the
head and tail will move. If we rotate it completely the head
and tail will always return to the right position. The Tails

can be made small as a hand toy, or if they are to be fixed to a background they can be made larger.

If the Tails turn out not to work properly at first it will almost certainly be because the parts are assembled too tightly. A little adjustment is probably all that will be necessary to free the movement and get them working properly. Because of the movement factor it will be useful to make the patterns on the Tails very simple and bold, like the stripes in the ones illustrated. This will make the visual effect of the movement more dramatic, because changes in direction will be pronounced and easy to see.

It will be interesting to watch friends and relations playing with this simple toy, and like the previous cats it might make a nice present for a friend in hospital, although it would have to be packed very carefully if it were to be sent through the post.

Tails can be fun made into cats, but they can also be made into other animals. This is again a matter for individual choice, and an opportunity for original experiment. The technique described here is the only thing which must be followed closely.

Blinkers

In making the previous toy we have been playing with card, and we can go on adapting and developing it in different ways. We can also, as we have seen in previous exercises, stay with the shape—in this case the cat—and we can try to experiment with it in other ways.

With Blinkers we must again look closely at the compared illustrations. The cats in Fig. 74 are the same as the cats in Fig. 75—but there is a difference. In Fig. 74 they have their eyes open, but not in Fig. 75. If we look very closely at the cats, comparing them again, we will also notice that the tongues have changed position. It is the movement of the tongue from side to side which allows us to open and close the eyes of the cats.

In Fig. 74 when the eyes are open the tongues are in the vertical position. Looking more closely at the tongues in Fig. 75, we will see that they have moved to the side, as though the cats were licking their lips.

The simple mechanism for the Blinkers is illustrated in the diagram Fig. 76. To make a Blinker it is necessary to cut two pieces of card: a body shape *A*, and a separate tongue and eye shape *B*.

Fig. 74 Blinkers . . .

Fig. 75 . . . and Blinkers.

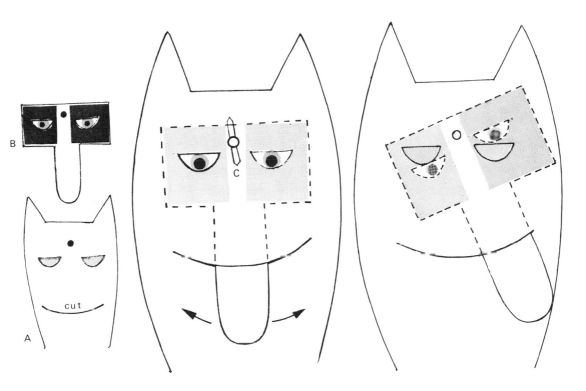

Fig. 76 Mechanism for Blinkers.

The body shape *A* can be cut as any shape but it must have a curved slot cut as shown, and must also have cut away semi-circles for the eyes.

The second piece of card *B* must incorporate a tongue at the bottom centre of a rectangle. The rectangle will also have on it eyes which are surrounded with darker areas of plain colour.

If we look at our own, or anyone else's eyes, when making these we will see that the eyeball is light with a dark pupil and iris at the centre. In any work we do with eyes included it is useful to remember this, because if we make the eyes right it helps to give character to the shape and to bring it to life.

The eye and tongue shape *B* must correspond to the shape of the body so that it can be hidden behind at *C*. To make sure of this it is best to cut the body first, making the openings for the eyes and the slot for the tongue. This can then be placed over the second piece of card before cutting it.

If the position of the eyes is drawn in outline through the holes in the top shape, and if the slot is marked as a line on the under shape, it should be easy to remove the card and cut the shape as shown. The tongue must be long enough to extend well below the slot, and the rectangle carrying the eyes should not extend beyond the sides of the body shape. The eyes and dark patches indicated by the toned areas can now be filled in.

When the two shapes are together with the tongue protruding through the slot in an upright position, a fixture can be made at C. This can be made with a paper fastener pierced through both shapes and opened at the back, so that sideways movement of the tongue will remove the eyes from the cut openings in the front shape and replace them with the plain coloured part of the background. This plain colour on the background shape must be above and below the eyes so that it will appear when the tongue is moved either to the left or to the right.

The fixture should in this case be firm and tight so that the eyes open and close only when the tongue is moved, unlike the previous cats when a totally free movement was needed.

This is a simple mechanism which, once it is understood, can be adapted to many other shapes. The witch, for example, might be interesting to look at, and it should be possible to work out for ourselves what makes her open and close her eyes.

The final effect of the Blinkers can be made slightly more unexpected and interesting if the head of the paper fastener is hidden from view. This has been done on the cats by applying a separately cut nose which has been decorated with a second shape in contrasting colour and which has been stuck at the top only, instead of all over. If the nose is only stuck at the top it will be loose where it rests on the fastener and will not interfere with any movement. The witch has her fastener hidden by the decorated paper hatband.

Blinkers are possible in the shape of many animals or humans, but they can, of course, be viewed only from the front. Like the Tails in the previous exercise they can be made as simple hand toys or they can be fixed to a background.

It might be interesting to have a friendly Blinker in a bedroom and to wake him—or her—each morning when we get up. If we make the Blinker ourselves we can choose any animal we like. A circular shape could be brightly patterned as a curled up snake, and it could have a forked tongue. We can make Blinkers as cats or dogs, but for this toy we can make a pet of any animal we like. We could also have our own human Blinkers: witches with patterned socks, clowns with big boots, or perhaps with a large patterned tie which could be moved instead of the legs.

If we had some Blinkers in the classroom we could have many different sorts of fun. We could make ourselves as Blinkers, and when we were working well we could have our eyes open. When we were not working quite so well we could be made to shut our own Blinker's eyes. We might have to work a bit harder then so that we could get our Blinker's eyes open again.

We might have a family of class Blinkers who would have to have their eyes closed at nights and opened in the mornings. There are many things we can do with Blinkers, and there are many different ones waiting patiently to be made by us.

Surface Treatments

In previous exercises we will have seen that even with our paper and card kept flat we can find any number of exciting possibilities for playing with the material. The shapes and patterns we cut and use will depend less on an ability to draw and more on the way we look and see the shapes around us. But the time will come, as we work, when we will be ready to learn new techniques and to use them in various exciting and new ways.

There is no specific or set order for learning techniques. What we can aim to do is to extend our understanding of the materials we use, and to explore their potential more fully. We have come a long way from the square we cut as our first exercise, but we can go back to it for a brief moment now and look at it in a new way. Besides looking at its shape we can now look at its surface.

When we start with paper or card the surface is flat, but it can be treated in various ways. In previous exercises we painted or stuck cut patterns on it. We can now explore two new possibilities. We can cut into the surface and raise parts of it. Or we can raise the surface by adding other shapes to it.

For some of this work we will need to use a knife as well as scissors, but this should not put us off. There are many good and cheap craft knives on the market, and it is not difficult to get one of the type which has blades which can be taken out and replaced. For a cutting surface any cheap card can be used and re-used until it has to be turned over and used again on the reverse side. It is possible to tell, by the way a surface interferes with the cuts, when the card is too pitted and rough for any further use. It can then be easily replaced.

When using a knife or any edge tool it is obviously necessary to treat the cutting edge with care, and to make sure that at all times, even if the knife should happen to slip there would be no chance of its causing any injury. This is a simple rule—the only one we have in paper play. The hand holding the paper to be cut must always be behind the blunt edge of the knife. The blade must never cut towards the holding hand. A useful point to remember also is that when we cut any surface with a knife it is better to make a number of cuts using slight pressure, rather than to try cutting at one go. When we put too much pressure on a knife we can easily lose control of it.

Any paper or card surface can be made visually interesting by cutting into it and raising the shapes cut. Various types of cut are possible, but we will find that the simplest ones still remain the most effective. If we can master the rectangular, pointed and curved cuts (Fig. 77), we will find these more than adequate in our later work. In this diagram the cut is shown as a continuous line. The dotted lines indicate how the shapes can be folded up from the surface.

The scale of any cuts we use will appreciably alter the material we are working with. Small cuts will enrich a surface without changing the original shape, but cuts can

Surface Treatment by Cutting

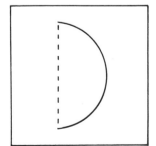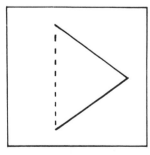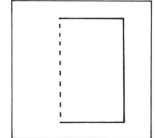

Fig. 77 Cuts for surface treatment can be simple.

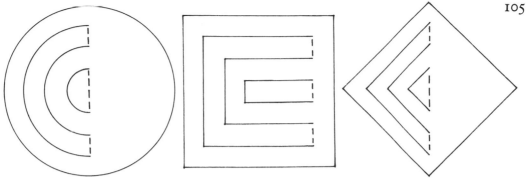

Fig. 78 Surface cuts can be large.

be varied in size right up to the point where they will actually change the shape.

The larger surface cuts shown in Fig. 78 will allow parts of the whole to be folded right across the shape. This might be tried as an exercise in cutting and the results exploited as hanging shapes in Fig. 80. The exercise will tell us a little more about the way paper can be used visually, and will provide opportunities for practice in measuring and cutting.

The illustration of these cuts applied to a square (Fig. 79) is not suggested as an exercise. It is included as an illustration of the way surfaces can be changed by cut treatments.

In the top line a rectangular cut is used throughout, but in various different ways. Starting with simple cuts at the left, the cutting and folding—in this technique folding implies slightly raising the surface—develops through various size and placing arrangements. The visual result of raising the cut parts is to alter the tone on their surfaces, and to contrast their shapes against the darker areas of the cuts.

The same treatment is repeated in the next two rows with triangular and curved cuts. The straight cuts are, of course, easier to make than the curved ones because a ruler or metal edge can be used as a guide. But the ability to cut freehand, both in straight and curved cuts, is a skill we should aim to develop. It will be interesting to see it grow as we practise.

Cut and raised patterns can be applied freely to any part of a surface but, like the examples illustrated, they can be measured and organized in geometric patterns.

106 Where measuring is carried out before cutting, marking can be done with pencil on the reverse side of the material. Folding is never difficult because the lines to be folded are invariably very short. Scoring—the technique of lightly marking the surface with a knife along the line to be folded—can be used, but it is not likely to be necessary.

Fig. 79 Surface treatments have different applications.

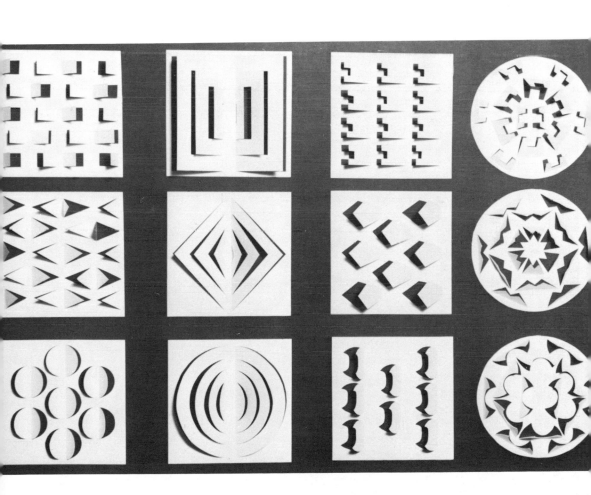

Fig. 80 Surface cuts can change the whole shape.

Low Relief Stars When we cut and raise a pattern of shapes on a flat surface it is no longer flat. The surface now has a textured or low-relief quality, and we can now begin to use this technique in our work.

In an earlier exercise (Fig. 65) we discovered how to make simple six-pointed stars. We might now investigate cutting their surfaces in various ways and raising more form in the shapes. There are many ways we can apply this technique to a star shape, and some of these are suggested in Fig. 81. The cuts are continuous lines, and the folds are indicated by dotted lines.

Fig. 81 Surface treated stars can be varied.

If the stars are cut in a silver-faced card they can be put together in twos with patterned papers inserted between them as in Fig. 82. This pattern will be visible when the cut shapes are raised on the surfaces of the stars.

Fig. 82 The stars will reflect light on the raised parts.

In the star mobile illustrated in Fig. 82 some of the stars have been stuck together point to point, and others have been positioned so that the points of one star are between those of the other. In this way it is possible to make a twelve-pointed star from the triangle template used in the original.

Where silver or gold faced card is used, the surfaces will reflect light and colour from any close source, especially on the raised parts of the shapes, and interesting contrasts will occur as the mobile moves.

The cut surface treatment of the stars is assisted by the symmetrical quality of the original shapes, and it is easy to make decisions about where to place the cuts (Fig. 81). But any shape we like to make can have various surface treatments.

Low Relief Birds

The birds in Fig. 83 begin, as cut shapes should, by being simple. But in the illustration the body is cut and exploited in various ways with curved or straight cuts. In these examples the cuts are large enough to allow shapes to be folded outwards at both sides, taking the birds from the flat shape to the beginnings of three-dimensional form.

In the top shape triangular cuts allow one wing to be folded outwards on one side, and one on the other. In the next shape a triangular cut is made again through the centre, so that one half of its shape can be folded at each side. In the third shape, the cuts are curved; and in the lowest shape they are rectangular. The lowest shape is further developed in Fig. 84. In this close-up of the shape we can see that the technique of cut surface treatment can be combined with applied pattern. In this example the stripes and spots are arranged to complement or add to the effect of the raised parts of the shape. The raised parts are folded to both sides to add more form to the shape. This form would be particularly visual as the bird revolved, and the patterning would have to be added to both sides of the shape.

It is interesting to note how a simple shape like the bird, which is no more than a semi-circle with a neck and head, can be made lively by the use of simple paper techniques which are well within the scope of our work at this stage. Similar treatments could be tried on any of the shapes we have previously experimented with, or any new shapes we might have found for ourselves.

Fig. 83 Surface cuts make many simple forms possible.

Fig. 84 Cut and folded surface treatment can be combined with applied pattern.

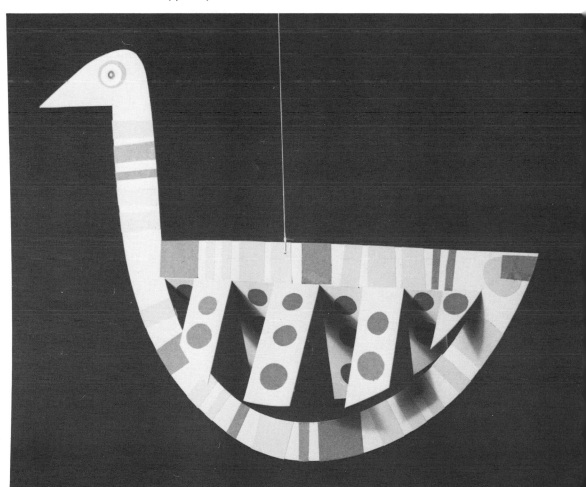

The technique of surface treatment by cutting and folding is simple and quickly learned. From this technique we can go on to explore the possibilities of surface treatment by the addition of other shapes.

If we start with the square again as a convenient shape we can see how this can be enriched (Fig. 85) by this technique. The squares shown have simple shapes added and folded upwards from the surface in various ways. In the top example, triangles have been cut with a sticking flap included. The added shapes can be left plain or they can carry their own cut treatments like those shown.

An extra advantage of the added shapes is that they can be cut and applied to a background in different colours. This will add a new contrast between the background and the shapes added to it.

In the centre row of the illustration, circles have been cut and folded vertically through the middle, and one half of the circle has been stuck to the background square. In this sort of treatment new background shapes begin to appear between the applied circles, and the circles themselves are seen as two quite different tones of colour.

As we know already there are many different shapes which can be cut for use in this way, and many different ways in which they can be folded and stuck. It is very much a matter of experiment and personal decision.

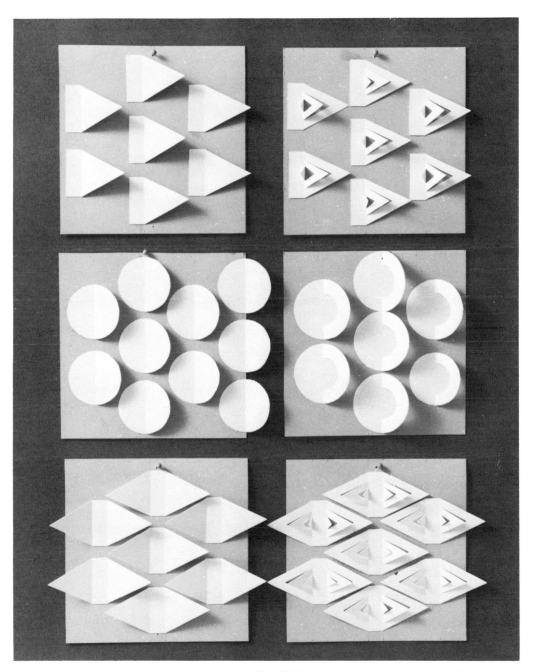

Fig. 85 Surface treatment can also be by addition.

When we looked at previous exercises with fish shapes we considered some of the various ways in which they might be cut and made in paper. We can now go on again to exploit them more fully.

The fish in Fig. 87 are simple shapes with surface treatments made with the addition of new shapes. The example at the top has been taken from the previous exercise, where cut circles in contrasting colour were folded through the middle and attached to the background with one half of the circle.

The elongated triangles in the second example are possibly more fish-like. The triangles, again like those in the previous example, were folded across the base to make a rectangular sticking seam, and their visual effect has here been explored more fully with a central line of holes made with a paper punch.

For neatness and ease of working, these triangles or any overlapping shapes stuck as closely as this, should be applied with a sticking sequence which starts at the back or most hidden shape. Each new shape which is added can then overlap the one already stuck.

In any of the examples shown it can be assumed that shapes will be added to both sides of the fish. These will give the original flat shapes both bulk and form so that as they turn an interesting form will always be visible.

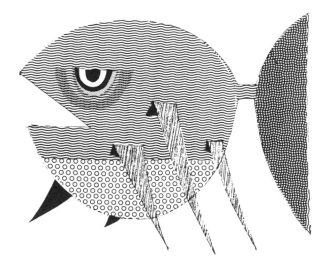

Fig. 86 Added surface shapes can lead to free-standing sculpture.

Fig. 87 Familiar shapes can be enriched with the techniques.

An interesting feature of this type of form development through added shapes is that it can be used to make free-standing sculptures. The shapes added to the side of a flat cut will stand out and act as props or supports (Fig. 86), making it possible to stand the shape as a simple three-dimensional sculpture. We might try this on the fish with different shapes added. Applied semi-circles, for example, would allow us to stand the shape but it would lean over at an angle. If the semi-circles in the bottom example (Fig. 87) were applied sideways with the curve as the lower edge the fish would not only stand as a free sculpture but it might also work as a simple rocking toy.

Rockers, which can be easily made as moving toys are an extension of the way form can be developed by adding to a surface. To demonstrate this we can cut two identical circles in card. If we use a pair of compasses to make the circles there will be a small hole at the centre of each of them. A line drawn through this point across the circle will divide it into two halves. If this line is scored slightly and folded, the two circles can be stuck together at their top halves (Fig. 88). The lower halves can then be opened at A, so that the joined circles will stand as shown. The joining of these two circles will make a free-standing form which can be rocked and which can be made into a simple moving toy, as in the illustration. It can be made either animal or human and can have its own special type of pattern treatment (Fig. 89).

Rockers

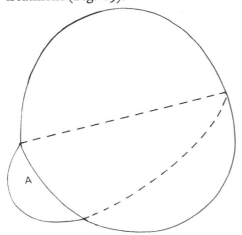

Fig. 88

Fig. 89 Rocker.

Flat Animal Shapes

There is a point worth noting at this stage in our work. When we put the two flat shapes together to make the Rocker, we were able to make a free-standing form. We should not let this opportunity pass without seeing if it is possible to explore the potential more fully.

If we cut a simple animal shape in card we can make it stand if it is cut twice. The two shapes must be exactly the same, and they must be stuck together at the top only, so that the lower part of the body can be opened out. The animals in Fig. 90 have been made to stand in this way. After sticking the two shapes at the top it has been possible to splay the legs open slightly so that the animals will stand unsupported.

Fig. 90 Two shapes put together will make a free-standing form.

Almost any animal shape can be made in this way, and any of them can be further treated with painted decoration or with the addition of some other material. String and wool are easy to get, and are very suitable for treatment of the animals, especially when they are frayed to add bulk to the flat surfaces on both sides.

A range of different animals made in this way might make an interesting project. The card could be collected from salvaged packaging, and string or wool could probably be collected from friends and relations. It could take the form of a zoo or a circus, or the animals could be made in pairs for a toy Noah's Ark. We might make a toy farm of recognizable animals, or a train of desert camels. In this age of space interest they could also be made in imaginary shapes to represent space creatures, in which case they could be decorated with all sorts of unexpected materials. If the card is firm enough we might make large prehistoric monsters with their exciting sounding names: diplodocus, triceratops and the well-known tyrannosaurus. If the card shapes are well pasted on the outside they can be made to look suitably rough and textured with a papier mâché treatment of pasted tissue paper.

Low Relief Butterflies

The addition of shapes to a surface can be combined with both cut and patterned treatments. In the butterfly mobile (Fig. 91) simple symmetrically cut shapes have been explored with various treatments. In some cases the shape itself has been cut and folded, and in others new shapes have been added with their own folds. These are all combined in one mobile with some drawn and painted surface treatment and with some patterned paper additions.

As we develop different skills it will be natural at times to combine the techniques. In this book they are separated and presented individually so that they can be understood. But they will all come together ultimately in any of our more advanced work if their combination adds to the effect of the end product.

Fig. 91 Added shapes can
be combined with other
surface treatments.

Now that we are beginning to move from flat shapes to ones which have form of their own, we have a wide range of possibilities open to us. We can, for example, now add features which have their own form.

The mobile of round faces in Fig. 93 is familiar from earlier exercises; but in this example, although they have some added decoration which is flat, they also have form in some of their features. Their noses are all different: the top one has a cylindrical nose, the next one has a triangle folded through the middle. The third one has a semi-circular form and the lowest one a rectangular form. In some cases the shapes on the ears have also been stuck so that they are bent slightly outwards in low relief.

Often, when we add a formed feature to a background it will be possible to run a little adhesive down the form and to stick it in place. It will sometimes, however, be necessary to add sticking seams. The triangular nose would need seams included in the original shape (Fig. 92). These could be folded behind when the form is raised through its fold, and could be stuck on the background to make an invisible fixture.

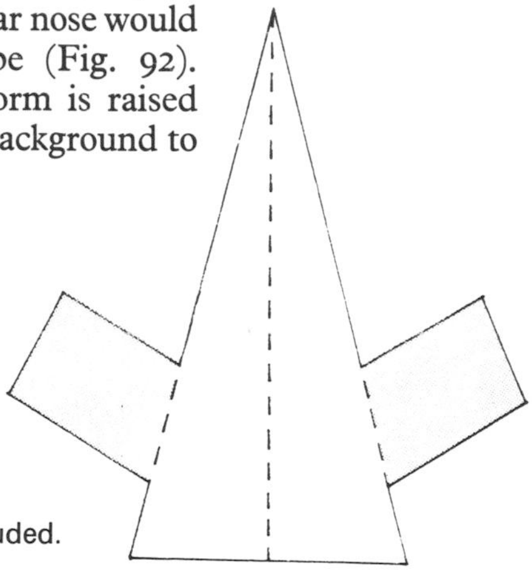

Fig. 92 Sticking seams can be anticipated and included.

The ability to anticipate and include sticking seams when we cut shapes can be developed as we work. It is a simple technique. In some instances when shapes are to be put together they will join at flat and easily fixed surfaces, but in others—like the triangular nose—the fixture could only be made at the edges and this would be inadequate.

Before cutting any shape which is to be added to another it is useful to consider how the fixture will be made. A sticking seam, folded away behind the shape and impact glued, is usually enough to hold any paper or card form to a background. It also has the added advantage of being invisible. Wherever possible its use should be anticipated and included in shapes to be cut.

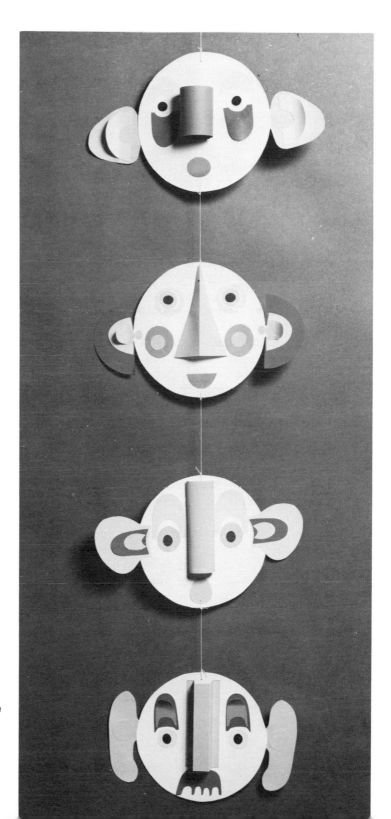

Fig. 93 Faces can have low relief features.

In previous exercises we have folded and added small shapes to a background, but the folding of paper for visual effect gives us many opportunities to play with textures on a surface.

If the folds are organized and controlled, a plain sheet of paper can be made to change its appearance dramatically. The examples in Fig. 94 illustrate only three of many different ways of folding interest into a piece of paper.

Most of us are familiar with the feel and appearance of corrugated card of the type used in packaging, and this is often a rewarding source of material to work with. It is similar in effect to the folds which we can make ourselves. We might remember here that many of the exercises already considered could be enhanced with the addition of corrugated card shapes as surface treatments. This is now available in a number of different colours, but it is also possible to paint or dye it any colour we want. A mobile of fish with corrugated card sides might make an interesting new visual experience for us, or we might try some bird shapes—some owls perhaps—with corrugated fronts. The visual effect of corrugation is rich and interesting because there is a play of light over the curves on its surface, but similar effects can be created deliberately by folding paper in different ways.

The most simple example of this is the well-known fan fold illustrated in the top shape Fig. 94. This effect can be made by freehand folding, or it can be made more accurately by marking equal distances along the top and bottom edge of the paper. For neat folding it is helpful to score the paper along the lengths of the folds, although it is only necessary to do this on one side. It is not necessary to alternate the scoring from side to side because in straight folds one can fold the paper with or against the score.

The fan fold illustrated here is often used to make a simple party decoration. If the folded sheet is pinched together tightly at the centre, with the folds together, and if this point is secured with a tightly tied thread, the top edges can be fanned out so that the top and bottom corners will meet at the sides. The result will be a circular shape with fan folds radiating from the centre.

In the two other examples the folds across the paper are slightly more complex. In these and other types of repeating surface folds it is necessary to work out the measuring procedure before starting the work. But this

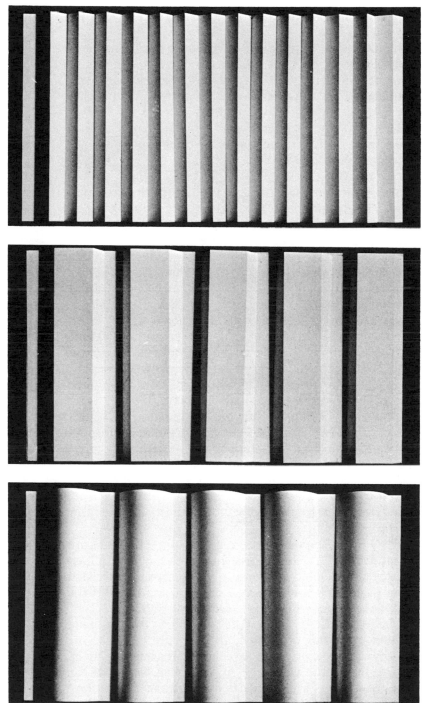

Fig. 94
Repeat Folding.

should not be difficult since they are all variations on the original fan fold.

In the lower example the curves will be flat to begin with, and each one will require the same measurement along the edges. To raise the pattern it would be necessary to stick the first sticking seam to the background, and then to raise the first curve which could be held in place by sticking the next flat section. It would be necessary to work progressively in this way across the sheet.

Repeat Folded Figures

Continuous folded paper can be used in many decorative ways. The hanging figures in Fig. 95 are simple cut-out shapes with added heads and hands. The features are also as simple as those used in previous exercises.

The figures themselves have been developed with the addition of cut paper strips which explore the possibility of various continuous folds. These figures, which are a little taller than this page, are made in a colour which contrasts with the strips, and are decorated on both sides. Although the applied decoration is very simple, the figures make a range of different shapes and contrasts as they turn. They could be made and hung singly, or they could be made up like the example illustrated into one of the mobile arrangements suggested earlier.

As we are looking at some of the potential of repeat folded paper, in this case as surface treatment, we might think a little of what actually happens to paper when we fold it into tightly repeating patterns. In the first place we make it visually interesting as the planes contrast between the folds. We also make it slightly springy when it is neither fully extended nor tightly folded. It is possible to use these two factors in simple decorations.

The clowns (opposite page 128) are simple shapes with repeat folded legs, and in one case with a repeat folded body. This is a good way of using up scraps of patterned paper left over from previous exercises, and some of the oddments of card which are usually lying about.

The folded papers in these shapes can be made freehand without measuring or scoring, and they can be of varying lengths made to suit the space available for hanging them.

If we make fun shapes with folded bodies or legs we can store them away for use as party or Christmas decorations. Folded and packaged neatly and sent through the post

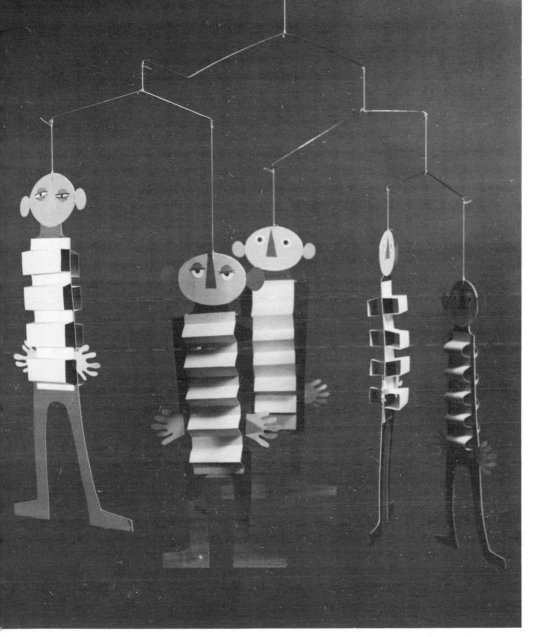

Fig. 95 Repeat Folded Figures.

they will make interesting surprise greetings as our friends take them out of their envelopes.

The repeat folds can be used in various shapes besides those shown on the clowns. Animals with repeat folded tails are obvious alternatives, and these can be made in many different shapes.

Low relief surface treatments can be folded to make a pattern, but like the noses in Fig. 93 they can be made up in many different ways. The Target Figures in Fig. 96 illustrate low relief treatment by separately added shapes, but in this instance they illustrate low relief treatment by separately added shapes.

Low Relief Figures

The figures have circular shapes at their centre in reducing sizes and in contrasting colours. These have been cut in card and have been fixed together with spacers in between them. These spacers are cut from an ordinary plastic tile of the sort used in interior decorating because this is both light and yet strong enough to hold the card. The glue used for sticking the spacers and card is a polymer adhesive (PVA) which is now generally available in the form of a white opaque liquid.

The visual effect of the separated shapes is interesting, and the simple technique of using spacers opens out new opportunities in our work. In many earlier exercises some of the shapes used might be further exploited in this way.

When we cut paper for use in low relief treatments we might need to measure and mark it before we fold it. We might also need to measure on various different occasions.

Measurers

In Fig. 97 some of our earlier animal shapes and some simple pattern shapes are seen in a new application. In this exercise we can start again with a simple shape which we intend to use as the body of an animal—any animal we like. The ones shown are only examples of very many possibilities.

When we have cut and made a simple head shape we can now add it to the body, adding a paper or tile spacer between them. A strip of paper or card fixed to the background shape at the top and bottom will make a simple spacer. If it is fixed only at the top, like a hinge so that the lower part hangs loose, this can be attached to the head so that it will move slightly in a breeze. The animals illustrated all have noses with form established through the centre folds.

Figures can have repeat folded legs or bodies.

Fig. 96 Low relief Target Figures.

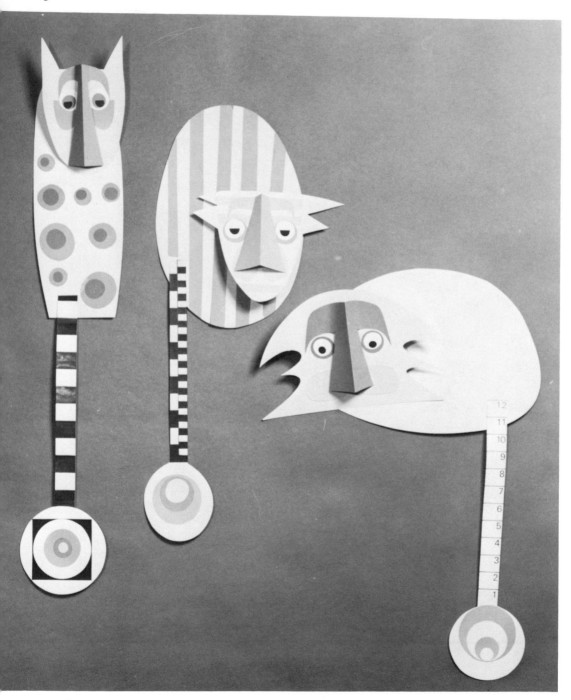

Fig. 97 Measurers.

To make the animals into Measurers we must develop
the tails as simple rulers. A strip of card, measured and cut
carefully, must be marked off accurately into measured
units. An ordinary ruler must be used for this. This strip
can then be slotted into the body like a tail. It should be a
tight fit, and the slot cut in the body must be only slightly
wider than the tail itself. If the shapes are handled with
care the ruler can be taken out and replaced when it is not
to be used for measuring.

In the cat at the left of the picture the body is long and
thin so that the tail can be hidden away completely except
for the patterned shape at its tip. If it starts like this as a
wall hanging—perhaps in the classroom where some of our
work might be concerned with measuring—the cat's tail
might be made to grow an inch every day. This could be
done just for fun, or it could be a way of familiarizing us
with simple measurement.

If we need a sounder reason for growing the tail we might
consider marking it like that of the tiger in the middle.
This tail is marked off both in inches and in centimetres,
so that every day, as we grow the tail an inch, we will be
able to compare this in metric measurement. The com-
parison might help us to an awareness of the relationship
between the two types of measurement.

The final tail in the illustration is measured and marked
off clearly in neat numbers. These have been applied with
figures from a rub-down sheet of the sort one can now buy
from some stationery suppliers. They are produced by
various manufacturers, and when they are available they
are a pleasure to use. But freehand numbers can be put on
carefully and the Measurers will still be worth using.

It might be interesting to make a Measurer with a yard
or a metre tail, so that we can grow it by stages and learn
about its length and what it is made up of. If we are younger
we might make a one yard tail and see how many days it
takes, pulling it an inch a day, before we pull the tail right
off. It is still playing with paper.

If we can cut into the surface of a paper to make it visually interesting, we should also be able to cut into the edge of a shape.

In a previous exercise (Fig. 59) we touched on the possibility of cut edge treatment, and reference was made to the variety of ways, over and above the normal saw edge type of cut, which might be possible.

There is a further interesting potential in the technique of edge cutting and folding a shape.

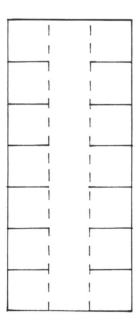

Fig. 98 Simple edge cuts.

If we take a rectangle of paper or thin card—about a third of the size of this page—and if we make simple parallel cuts on two opposite sides as in Fig. 98, we can fold the edge into a pattern. If we make the folds on the dotted lines we can fold one shape one way at a right angle to the original, and one shape the other way, repeating this pattern down the length of one side and then up the other. If the shapes on the two sides are folded in opposite directions the visual pattern will be pronounced and interesting. Variations on this pattern are possible if the horizontal arrangement of the cuts is changed. These can be varied to slope upwards or downwards, and if the same folding pattern is maintained the results will be visually quite different (Fig. 99).

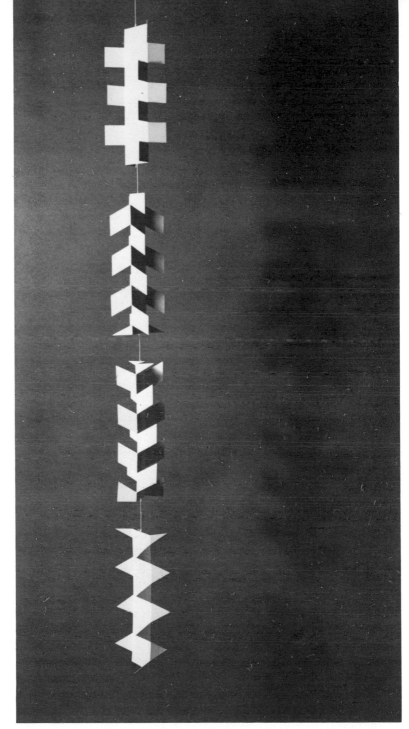

Fig. 99 Variations in edge cuts are possible.

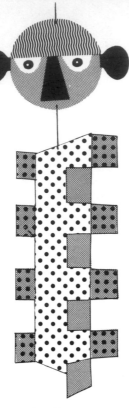

Fig. 100 Edge cut Fun Hanger.

An edge cut shape can be developed decoratively in various ways. A rectangle treated in this way, and with some surface decoration can be combined with a simple face to make a fun hanger (Fig. 100). We can play with the potential as we like; starting with any shape and putting colour and decoration on it before we cut and fold the edge. We can then combine the shape with a face at the top or bottom, or both; and we can arrange them together in a mobile. It is this sort of cut and folding treatment which, as in Fig. 99, will begin to make interesting and changing background shadows as the shapes revolve.

Edge Cutting and Decorating

When we have started to experiment with cut and folded edges on a shape we begin to find ourselves working more and more away from the flat shape. We might now investigate this deliberately. If we start at a familiar point, at one of the better known shapes, we will find that by working at its edge we can make any number of simple forms. As we have seen already a shape is often a great deal more than it at first seems.

In Fig. 101 the diagram starts with a rectangle at the top. The continuous lines on the other rectangles must be cut, and the dotted lines are for folding. It will be seen that in no case is any part of the rectangle being removed. We are concerned with some of the forms within a known shape. If we remove part of it, it will be a different shape.

Fig. 101 Cutting and folding a familiar shape has many possibilities.

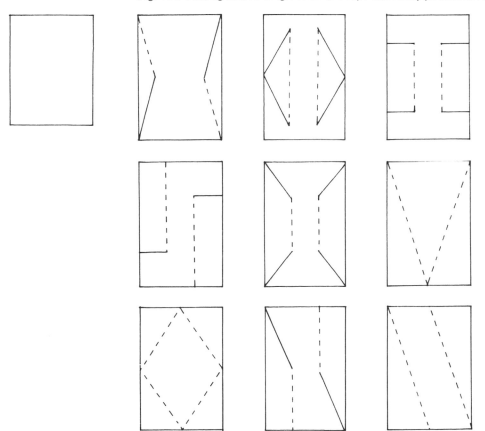

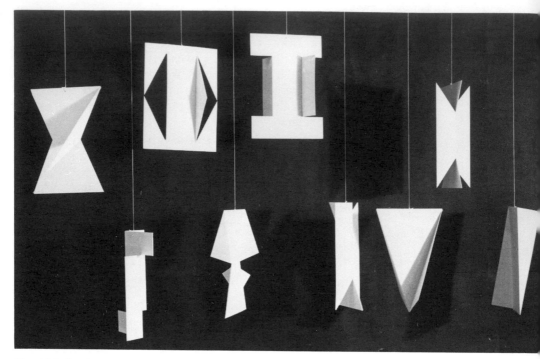

Fig. 102 Cutting and Folding makes entirely new shapes.

The rectangles, cut and folded exactly as shown are illustrated in Fig. 102, in which they are hung in a great variety of new forms. It is interesting to consider, since the rectangles are suspended, how these new forms will go on making even more new forms as they turn again and again through 360°.

It is a good simple exercise to start with some rectangles, or squares if there is a preference for them, and to treat them, either as some of those shown or in any of the many different ways which are not illustrated, and to see how many new forms we can find. The cutting and folding processes will be useful exercises in measuring and in the development of simple manual skill.

We will further extend our visual experience by looking at the shapes and by seeing them change. The remarkable thing is that again, as in our earlier experiments with the flat square, there are so many form variations possible that it would take a very long time—much longer than any one of us could possibly afford—to adequately explore the potential.

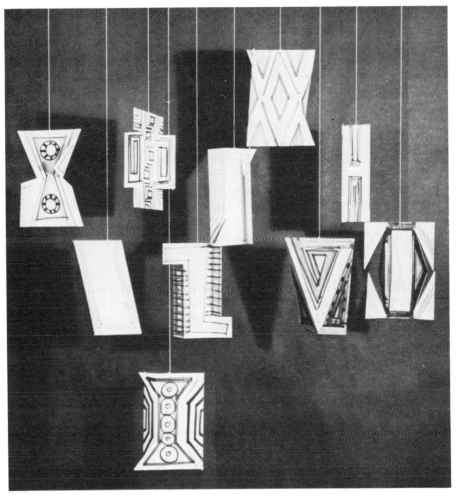

Fig. 103 The new shapes can be changed with pattern.

We can extend this exercise again by considering the effect of decorative treatments on the planes and surfaces made from the rectangles in Fig. 103. When we consider how many different visual experiences we can create from a simple rectangle, cut and folded in various ways and then treated with any of the surface decorations possible, we might begin to comprehend some of the enormous scope of the material we are using; and we might appreciate that, no matter how long we go on playing with it, we are never likely to exhaust its potential. There will always be something else to discover.

When we pick up a piece of paper now we will probably no longer see it as a simple rectangle, and a straight cut edge will probably not seem anything like as definite as it used to. We know that any piece of paper can be played with and manipulated into a whole range of new possibilities, and if we are interested we will look for new ways of exploring some of them.

The shapes in Fig. 104 started as a sheet of white card. This was measured and cut into ten rectangles, which was a convenient way of dividing it. These rectangles were then given cut and folded treatments at their sides. They were also decorated on the surface. A suitable ten-letter word was then found and each card was given a letter from it. The process was then repeated on the other side, with the word in the reverse order—compare the first letter in Fig. 105.

When the cards are strung and hung together with the movement stopped the word can be read. But when the shapes are allowed to move in their own way (Fig. 105) it will become possible to pick out new words from various combinations of letters as they appear.

The Word Mixer is a simple exercise. In this instance it is made with cards which have edge treatments, but almost any horizontal arrangement of shapes can have letters superimposed on the patterns. The prospect of Word Mixers is not likely to attract anyone unless there is already some interest in words or in word games.

A ten-letter Word Mixer like the one shown is a long example of this simple word game, but the length can be

Fig. 104 A sheet of card can be cut and rearranged . . .

adapted to suit any particular instance. Shorter words can be used, or perhaps names.

The game can actually be made more interesting by linking words with particular sorts of pattern treatments. The letters of a word like WATER can have a suitable coloured and patterned background (see Fig. 29). Other words can be investigated and tried: whirling, spotted, wrinkled, linear, autumnal, striped, tinted. There are many words in our language which tell us something about the appearance of things, and which—if we made mobiles of them—might lead us to experiment with an entirely new range of colours and patterns.

It is possible also to play interesting games with Word Mixers. The most obvious of these is one in which we find new words appearing as the shapes move. This could be an exciting and perhaps noisy game for a group. Another game might be one in which, after moving for a time, the Word Mixer is stopped and the letters are written down in the order seen on the stopped mobile. These letters must then be used as the initial letters of words in a complete sentence.

To make it more difficult, while the sentence is being decided on and written the mobile can be started again, and then stopped once more—for another sentence which must continue on from the previous one. A ten-letter mobile like the one illustrated would probably be too difficult for this game, but a shorter Mixer with two teams playing will really cause some interest and thinking about words.

Fig. 105 . . . as a Word Mixer.

Folding is now one of the ways in which we can make paper do some of the things we want. A flat piece of paper which will only lie down can be made to stand upright if we fold it through a vertical; and if the paper is not too flimsy we can turn it on its side, so that with the fold in it will stand in a ʌ-shape, like a roof.

We have already looked at some of the decorative or textured effects we can get with Repeat Folding. We can now begin to examine the fold as a deliberate technique in three-dimensional modelling. The single fold allows us to make the paper stand upright, but this in itself has many different possibilities.

A square of paper can be made to stand upright with one or any number of vertical folds introduced into it. It will also change its appearance slightly as the number or arrangement of folds is varied. There will be different planes contrasting in light and dark tones, and there will be various cast shadows on some of the planes (Fig. 106). The effects of folding, and some of the ways in which folds can be used deliberately are worth investigating.

Fig. 106 Experiment in change through straight folding.

Number Knockers

We have used cats before, but this time we can use them with a fold included so that they will stand unaided.

The cats in Fig. 107 are for knocking over. They are a simple form of skittle which is easy to make. They can be knocked down with a ball rolled along the ground, or they can be used in a game which requires a little more skill— the sort of game in which they have to be bowled over with a ball swinging on a length of string.

Fig. 107 Number Knockers for knocking over.

The ordinary skittles are easy. All we need is a ball and a free space on the floor. To make the swinging ball version of the skittles, a broom-handle or any suitable length of wood can be tied to the leg at one corner of a table, so that as much of it as possible extends upwards above the table surface. A ball, tied around with thin string and then attached by a length of string to the top of the pole, can be swung in a circle across the table surface, around the pole or in various backward or forward movements. Care must be taken to see that the length of the string makes it possible to swing the ball just across the surface of the table. To play it is necessary to knock down a number of cats and to add up the scores of the numbers shown. In either method the Number Knockers must have a score number included somewhere in their decoration.

In the game illustrated the cats are roaring out quick decimal numbers for mental arithmetic exercises. A ball swung across the group might knock a number of them over, and the sum of their numbers would be the player's score.

This is a simple game we can make for ourselves, and we can include numbers of any sort we like. Numbers similar to those shown might be much too simple for some players, but the selection of numbers for use on the Knockers is a matter of choice. If these are really too simple we can mark them with larger or more complex amounts, although—at a quick glance—what is the total score if all the cats are knocked down at one go?

Number Knockers can be fun. They can be animal or human in shape, or monsters created from our own imaginations. For those of us who dislike mental arithmetic exercises, Monster Knockers might be a satisfying project, and knocking them over convincingly—which will take a little skill—might add to the fun. Once again we might learn as we play.

The knockers can be left out after use if they are suitably decorated, or they can be folded flat and stored away while we experiment perhaps with other folded shapes.

The fold through the centre of a paper or card will allow us 143 to cut a whole range of interesting symmetrical shapes. If we look at a face it is symmetrical. With a fold in the paper we can cut a mask or we can cut a Party Nose.

We have seen that if we take a nose and simplify it to a triangle, and if we add circles for the eyes, we begin to get close to the human face (see Fig. 55). A triangle and circles cut together on the fold, and with simple added features, eyebrows and perhaps a moustache, will make a fun Nose for party time (Fig. 108). The shapes should again be simple and uncluttered, and the fold should be left through the centre so that there is some form in the Nose when it is worn. Flaps can be included in the cutting process at the sides as shown, so that rubber bands or string can be added to make the Noses wearable.

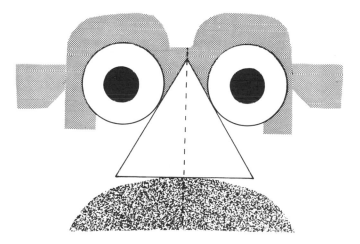

Fig. 108 A Folded Face can be . . .

The examples illustrated in Fig. 109 are all based on the triangle and circle shape with simple variations at the nose or eyebrows. The decoration illustrates some of the effective potential of adhesive tapes, either plain coloured or metallic. This is beginning to be available in an increasing range of colours, and can be applied in bold patterns direct from the roll.

Fig. 109 . . . party Noses.

Striped or spotted, or decorated in any way, Party Noses can be made quickly and easily, and can be part of the fun in the preparations for a party. It is necessary, of course, to punch small holes in the eyes for the wearer to see through. If a punch is not available, the holes can be pierced through the card with anything sharp enough, but this should be done with the Noses flat on the working surface.

Guests arriving at a party which starts with the handing out of Party Noses might be persuaded to wear them. Their reactions to each other, and to themselves, might be amusing.

Folded Stars In earlier exercises we might have made six-pointed stars from a single triangle (Fig. 65), and we might have developed these with cut surface treatments (Fig. 82). A different type of development is possible if we cut the stars flat as before, and now change their appearance by folding.

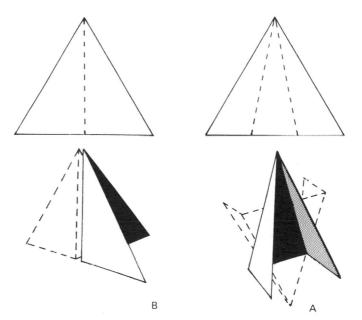

Fig. 110 The flat stars can be folded and put together.

Simple folds only are necessary: a single vertical fold through the centre, or two folds from the base to the point or apex of the triangle (Fig. 110). When the triangles are folded they can be glued together as shown in the diagram.

Fig. 111 Folded and joined stars become three-dimensional.

The star with two folds included (Fig. 110*A*) can be stuck neatly against one similarly folded. When these two stars are put together the form they make is three-dimensional. It can have simple added decoration in patterned paper or foil, and can be hung singly or in various arrangements like the right-hand example in Fig. 111.

The single fold stars can be assembled in fours to make a three-dimensional form. If they are first stuck together in twos (Fig. 110*B*), the units they make can be put together by reversing and sticking one to another as in *A*. The four-shape stars (left-hand example, Fig. 111) can also be decorated with simple foil and pattern shapes, particularly with foil if they are to be hung, because this will catch and reflect light as the stars move around.

Folded Shapes

There are many opportunities for playing with paper by folding it, and there are many ways of starting out to do so. The vertically folded cats suggested as Knockers might have more than one fold, or they might have different edge treatments making different shapes. These are based on the single fold shape (Fig. 106). Any of the other shapes in this illustration can be explored. The double fold, for example, at the opposite end can be further cut after folding (Fig. 112).

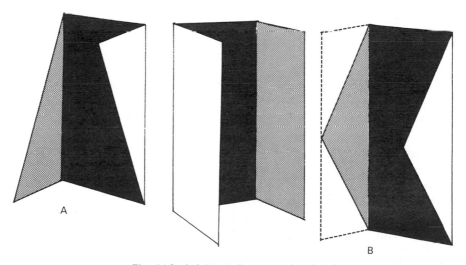

Fig. 112. A folded shape can be developed as a new shape.

When folded shapes are put together they tend, like the stars in the previous exercise, to make interesting forms. If we take this double folded rectangle, and if we make a number of them to begin with—they can be quite small— we will find it possible to marry them together into interesting paper forms. If we were to stick four of them together in the simplest plan view arrangement (Fig. 113) of two stuck together with one more added at each end, we would get a form with a number of sides and projections. This is illustrated in the upper form in Fig. 114.

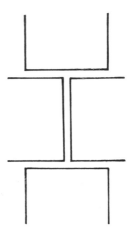

Fig. 113 One arrangement of the folded shapes.

This same arrangement is repeated in the middle two forms again, but in this case the sides of the original shape are cut. The upper form is made up with shapes cut from opposite corners (Fig. 112A), and the lower form from the shape cut as B.

These are simple and predictable arrangements, but the forms which result are interesting and can sometimes be used to make simple hanging or standing sculptures. The shapes making up the form can be cut in contrasting colours. They can be decorated in the usual way and can be hung in multiple arrangements.

The remaining form in the illustration is an experimental arrangement of the rectangle Fig. 112A. It is an example of the many unusual forms which can be made from a simple flat starting point.

Fig. 114 The fold will make new forms when shapes are put together.

This sort of exercise in which we can discover something new about shapes and their potential in folded arrangements might only appeal to the mathematically minded, but for those of us who like to sit quietly with pencil and ruler, exploring the possibilities of a few sheets of paper, there are many new forms waiting to be discovered, both with vertical folds and in other experiments.

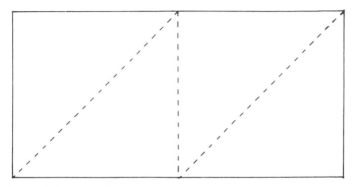

Fig. 115 A rectangle can be folded in one of many experimental ways . . .

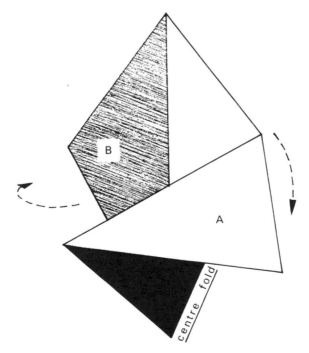

Fig. 116 . . .which will make a three-dimensional form.

We can experiment with the rectangle (Fig. 115). This is an experiment in folding a flat shape into a form, and then putting a number of the same forms together. The only skills required are the ability to cut a rectangle which is equivalent to two squares—two sides of the rectangle being twice as long as the others.

In place of the vertical fold we must now fold the rectangle as shown by the dotted lines in the diagram Fig. 115 across the middle, and then through the diagonals of the squares. It is important to establish the folding points and to make creases through the lines dotted.

The rectangle can now be folded into a three-dimensional form (Fig. 116). It must first be folded on the centre line, and the triangles *A* and *B* folded outwards as shown. The easiest way to make the form will be to look hard at the diagram Fig. 116; fold the paper through the centre line, holding it at the angle shown, and then fold the triangles in the directions of the arrows.

The form can be made permanent by sticking the overlap which remains at the centre fold after *A* and *B* are folded. It is a form which will now stand on any one of its seven sides, although it started as a flat rectangle with four sides. Once the folding has been understood the form can be made easily from any rectangle of the right proportions. It is an interesting exercise to decorate the rectangle when it is flat, especially with a line or geometric pattern, and to consider the way the lines change direction when the form is raised. A number of the forms can be hung separately as a mobile, or they can be combined together, one being stuck to the next, to make exiting new developments (Fig. 117). The multiple form illustrated might look complex and difficult in the illustration, but there is a surprising simplicity about the way a number of any one form can be married together. The individual units must be made up to start with, and must be glued as forms. After this there is a process of experiment and consideration, during which various arrangements can be tried. Once the development of a multiple form has started, the sticking process should be the same with each unit. It is, like the cutting and making of the units, a mathematical process.

When we have worked in the past we have done one thing, and then we have in most cases tried the same thing in an entirely different way.

The rectangle used in the previous exercise can, as a

Fig. 117 The form can be treated or combined in many ways.

further development of the experiment, be folded in a slightly different way to raise new forms. If we crease the rectangle this time as shown in the diagram Fig. 118, it can be folded to make the six-sided form in Fig. 119. This is again a very simple process. We crease the rectangle as shown, and then make three folds, with the triangles *A* and *B* opening outwards from the centre to make a flat square of their own. The triangle overlapping on the centre fold can be glued (dark tone in Fig. 119).

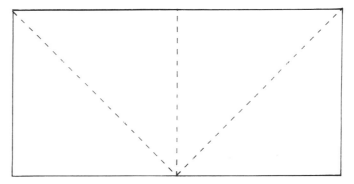

Fig. 118 Other folds are possible . . .

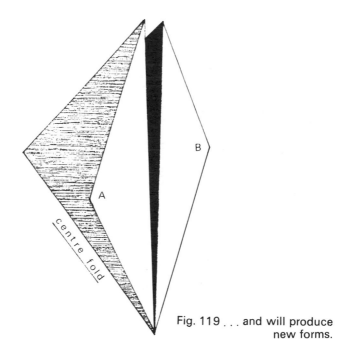

Fig. 119 . . . and will produce new forms.

Fig. 120 New forms make different arrangements possible.

The form made from this treatment of the rectangle is
explored in various ways (Fig. 120). The vertical arrangements will be simple to follow when there are a few forms
made up as single units. The circular developments will
again attract those of us who have patience and willingness
to work methodically, although they are not difficult. These
and many other forms can grow from the multiple arrangement of a number of these units. Because there are folds
included the forms will be surprisingly strong, and will
stand up to quite a lot of handling in the experimental and
making up stages.

But for those who are less methodical or patient we can
still find fun opportunities with simple folded shapes.

The Faster You Walk

This is perhaps a strange title for a folded paper shape.
But it is an interesting exercise in measuring, and in this
case—moving.

The rectangle used in the previous exercises can be cut
again, but this time it must be cut as two squares. These
should be cut in card or in thick paper, and they must, of
course, be equal.

Both squares can now be cut from the centre of one side
to the middle of the square (Fig. 121 *A* and *B*), and creased
on the dotted lines. It should be seen that when the creasing
is done as shown, one square will have the cut at the top
and the other in the lower part of its shape.

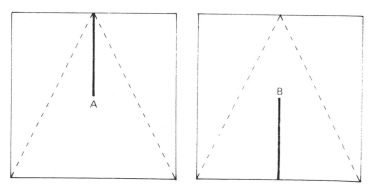

Fig. 121 Cuts for interlocking the squares.

When the cuts are made, the two squares can be interlocked at right angles by slotting one into the other. The creases will enable the top part of each square to be folded in the same direction (Fig. 122), in each case from the centre point to the bottom edge. The intention should be to make this a tight push fit so that the squares will remain interlocked at right angles, but if they do tend to go flat they can be held in the correct position with small strips of adhesive tape.

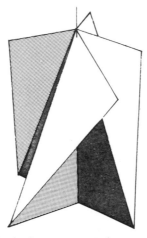

Fig. 122 The interlocked squares can have corners folded in the same direction.

The form which is made up with the folded and interlocking squares, Fig. 123 (outer examples) can be hung from a thread. It is interesting to make up and thread the form, and then to try walking with it. The faster it is walked, the faster the form will revolve.

This is a fun exercise to measure and make, and it can be decorated in many different ways to add to the effect of the movement. Things happen when colour is placed on a surface, and new things happen to the colour when the surface moves.

For those of us who enjoy measuring and cutting, this shape is shown in a slightly more complex development in the larger shape, centre of Fig. 123. In this example the folded treatment of the square is included at the top and bottom of two of the original rectangles, and these are then locked together. It is an exercise for those who like measuring. The rest of us can stay with the single fold Walkers.

Fig. 123 The Faster You Walk.

Three-dimensional Forms

We are now working, or if we are still light-hearted, playing in three-dimensional forms. We have arrived at this point almost inevitably, sometimes even by accident, because we have to fold paper when we set out to make things with it.

But we can be deliberate in our work in three-dimensions. We can set out to use forms which we know, and which we can control and exploit. There are many complex and ambitious forms which can be raised in paper, but there are also a number of simple basic forms. Like the familiar squares which started our investigations in shape and its development, these forms are recognizable and probably familiar to most of us. It should be possible for all of us to recognize these forms, to know how to construct them if necessary, and to appreciate how they can be used.

Fig. 124 There are various basic forms.

The forms illustrated in Fig. 124 are all made with thin card. They are not extraordinary, and we can find them all in day to day usage around us. Because a form has space inside it, we will find them mostly used as containers: as packages which contain things, or as buildings containing people. Some forms are, of course, not containers as such. When they are solid they usually have a specific purpose, like a building brick or a dice, but the forms which we make will be made up from the flat and will be hollow.

The diagrams which follow in this section and which illustrate the method of drawing, cutting and raising some of the simpler basic forms are included for those of us who want to make the forms for themselves but who need help to do so. Others will know how to make them, or will be satisfied to use forms which they can find ready-made. It is not essential to know how to make up the forms, and some readers will want to pass on to the more interesting opportunities for playing with them. Again there is no rule; it is a matter for personal choice and preference.

Cube At the beginning of this book we started with one of the simplest of shapes, the square. We can begin to consider form and its potential in exactly the same way—from a simple beginning. In this case the three-dimensional development of the square is the cube, the form which has six sides, all of them squares of the same size. It is easy to pick out the cube in Fig. 124.

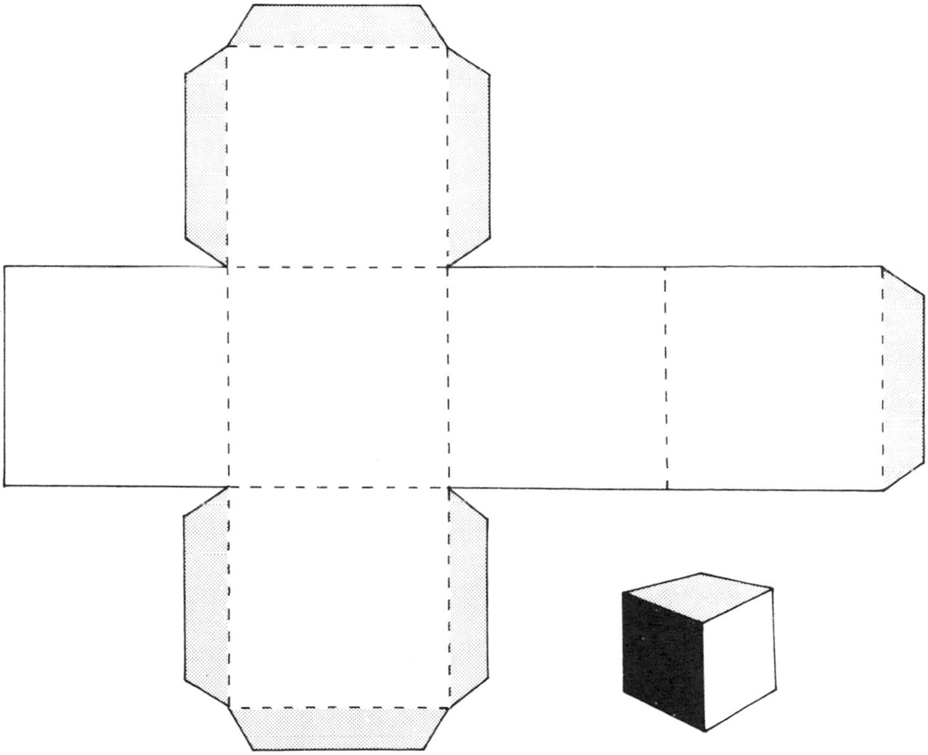

Fig. 125 Making the Cube.

In the diagram (Fig. 125), the squares which make the four sides of the cube are shown in a horizontal arrangement, with a sticking seam at one end. The top and bottom of the cube are shown as squares above and below one of the sides. They also have sticking seams, but these must be on all three sides.

If the form is going to be made neatly, and there is no reason why any one of us should not be able to do this, the measuring must be done as accurately as possible. Near enough is not good enough in this sort of work. The squares must be of exactly the same size, and the lines must be straight.

The size of the sticking seams is a matter of choice. For any cube which is dimensionally smaller than this page, seams of approx $1\frac{1}{2}$ cm or $\frac{3}{4}$ inch should be adequate.

The dotted lines in this and the other diagrams are the points at which the shape must be folded—also accurately —and should be gently scored so that the cube can be made up as cleanly as the one illustrated and as accurately as any of the boxes which come into the home almost every day.

After marking and cutting the shape, it is best to stick the four sides first. The top and bottom can then be stuck in any order.

It is possible, when we work three-dimensionally, that we will use open-ended forms like those in the centre of Fig. 126, in which case the top and bottom can be omitted from the cube in the original plan.

The cubes in Fig. 126 begin to suggest some of the potential of the made-up form. In the first place they can be made in various sizes. They can be made open-ended or closed. And they can be used as working surfaces for decorative treatments.

This takes us right back to our experiments at the beginning of the book. There is so much we can do on the cube. We can make new patterns on it in a variety of colours. Like the square we started with, there are un-limited possibilities.

Surface treatments of the cube are best done with the shape flat, after cutting and before sticking, and any work on the surfaces should, of course, be dry before the form is made up.

When we have cubes which can be treated on their various surfaces we have the opportunity for many simple sculptural experiments.

Fig. 126 Forms can be closed or open-ended.

In the example illustrated (Fig. 127) ten cubes of the same size are arranged one on top of the other as a single column. In this case the applied decoration on each cube makes an over-all effect when they are put together. The decoration is a two-colour measured treatment defined by straight lines at various angles. This is one of an enormous range of decorations possible, and since each cube has six faces, the illustration shows only one of the many different arrangements of placing which can be tried in the column.

In Fig. 128 the same squares are again arranged in a different grouping to create an entirely new sculpture. In this arrangement the staggered placing opens up new opportunities for light and tone differences, but is again only one of many arrangements possible.

The examples illustrated are not intended to be tried as

Fig. 127 Decorated forms can be put together in sculptural
arrangements.

Fig. 128 The forms can be rearranged.

exercises. They are merely intended to suggest the potential. With six faces on one cube, and the possibility for an
enormous range of surface treatments, the combination
of a number of cubes makes a simple type of movable
sculpture possible.

It would be enough as a simple exercise to start with
three or four cubes. These could be coloured on their
different surfaces or they could be in black and white, and
when they were finished and made up they could be considered in some of their various different arrangements.
It might be interesting to see, for example, how many
different arrangements and different visual effects could
be made with three cubes. They could have plain colour
decoration on their surfaces. They could have geometric
treatments like some of the earlier shape exercises. They
could have faces or numbers, even words. There are as
many opportunities for decoration and playing on the face
of a cube as there are on any piece of paper. And on the
cube, as we know, there are actually six faces!

We have already seen that a piece of paper can be treated
in many different ways, with applied treatments or with cut
surface treatments. We can now apply the techniques
suggested in earlier exercises to our work with three-
dimensional forms.

The surface treatment of the cubes in the vertical
mobile (Fig. 129) can be related back to the introduction
of the technique (Fig. 77). The cut surface treatment
applied in this instance to the faces of the cubes makes each
one a new form. When the cut shapes are raised from the
surfaces the forms become different visually as light
appears through the openings, and as the light sets up
more intense contrast with the darker tones inside the
form.

It is interesting in this example again to look at the
shadows on the background, and to consider how effective
these can be when they are cast by hanging and moving
forms. The complex surface treatment of the cube (Fig.
130) has been cut deliberately to explore the shadows it
would give. This is a more advanced treatment of the technique, and it would require careful measuring and cutting
to raise the surfaces of the cube as shown, but there are
many opportunities for experiment between this and the
previous simpler example. If the cube is measured accurately it must be possible to mark off the surface in any one

Fig. 129 Forms can have cut surface treatments.

Fig. 130 Complex surface treatments cut to explore light and shadows.

of many different ways, and to use the marks as guides for
experimental surface cutting. A single form such as this,
which has cut and raised pattern on its surfaces can be a
satisfying project to attempt. If it is made with care it can
be, like the example shown, an unusual result from an
ordinary flat paper beginning.

Square Prism If we take a cube and if we elongate it, keeping the top and
bottom square, we will have another three-dimensional
shape which is easy to make and which can be very useful
in our work. This form (Fig. 131) is a square prism. It
should not be difficult to see that in order to draw and construct it the sides must be equal rectangles, and that the
top and bottom must be squares with sides equal to the
width of the rectangle. Except for these differences in
dimensions, the drawing and making of the square prism
is exactly the same as that used to construct the cube.

Fig. 131 The square prism.

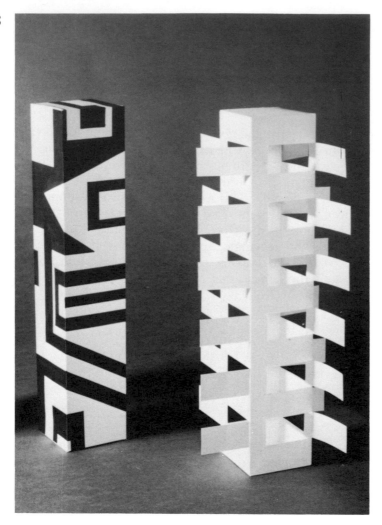

Fig. 132 The square prism with applied techniques.

The simple square prism, illustrated in Fig 131, can be exploited in many different ways. In the first example of Fig. 132 the prism has been decorated with a geometric surface treatment in black. This was done with the shape flat on the working surface, and was an exercise in free measuring and ruling. Because the pattern was developed over the whole surface it is different on every face of the prism, including the top and bottom, and various different visual experiences are possible by turning the standing form in different ways. This sort of free measuring exercise, where marks made across a surface are linked up in various ways, can be fun and can lead to new and unexpected patterns. The example shown has been carried out in black on white for maximum visual effect but any number of colour combinations are possible.

The second development illustrated is of a cut surface treatment, also undertaken as a measuring exercise. It looks complicated but the intervals are consistent, with each surface marked off in a ladder pattern of equal measurement. The marking was done on the back of the shape, and the cutting was done with a knife and a steel ruler. It was a process which required concentration and care, rather than great skill. But apart from these and the time required there is nothing specially difficult or ambitious in this or any other cut surface treatment.

The same prism is developed again in the plate opposite page 170. In the first case the circles and triangle of a previous exercise have been cut and included as a beak. These were cut with sticking flaps included so that the shape could be fixed easily to the form.

The form itself has been covered with patterned paper, and simple shapes have been cut and added as applied surface decorations. This is again a technique we have previously considered. The wings are simple shapes which have been curved by running an edge across one of the surfaces.

The clown has a simple applied face, ears which have been fixed with sticking flaps, and other decoration which would pose no problem to anyone.

The lion has a nose with form raised on a simple vertical fold. This is stuck flat at the eyebrows. The mane is fixed at the sides with sticking flaps and, as with the clown, various other pieces are cut and added for effect.

These treatments on a basic form must be well within

reach of any of us. There is nothing complicated about any one process. The important thing is to have the form to start with and to understand that one must work on the form as it is, using the simple techniques we know to make the statement. A bird or a clown or a lion can be drawn accurately by a competent draughtsman, using a line to suggest the shape. But we are working in a material which can be cut instantly into simple shapes. Whenever we work we can pick out simple essentials: the eyes and beak of the bird, the nose and ears and the bow-tie of the clown, the lion's mane, and we can put these on any basic form to make the thing we want. If we can work in attractive colours and patterns, and if we can decide on the simple essentials of the subject, we can make a basic form into anything we like.

Rectangular Prism

The square prism is a form with equal rectangles at all its sides, and with a square top and bottom.

If all the sides are not equal rectangles, if the front and back are the same, but different from the sides, we have a form known as a rectangular prism.

This will be very familiar to all of us because it is the form most commonly used in packaging. It is the form most commonly used, for example, for cereal and detergent packs, and can usually be found around the house waiting to be played with in some way.

To draw the rectangular prism it will be necessary to make all the sides the same height, but they will be different in width. The first one will be the same as the third, and the second will be the same as the fourth. The top and bottom must be rectangles which relate in size to the different sides. The easiest way to understand this is to take an empty package similar to the left-hand rear shape in Fig. 124, and to open it out carefully at the sticking seams.

There are so many of these shapes round every home that it might not even be necessary to make them up for oneself.

Square prisms can have many treatments.

Cylinder Faces with basic shapes.

Cylinders can become birds.

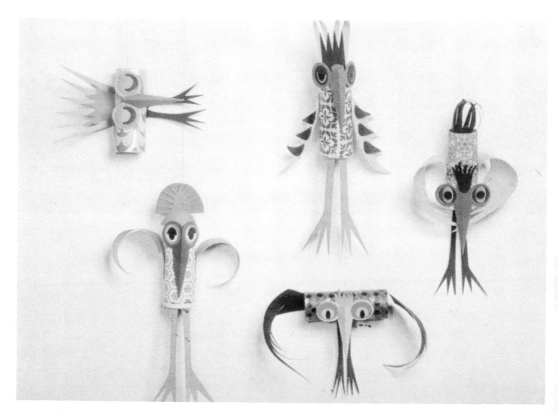

Flexibles The Flexibles (Figs. 133 and 134) are made up from detergent packs fixed together with ribbon and adhesive tape (Fig. 135) and then covered with wrapping paper. In the first example (Fig. 133), additional decoration has been drawn on with felt-tips, and the end shape has been given a simple eye to establish the front of the Flexible.

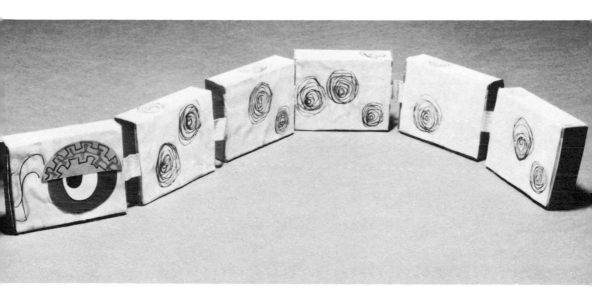

Fig. 133 Flexibles of rectangular prisms.

Fig. 134 The Flexibles can be made from salvaged packaging.

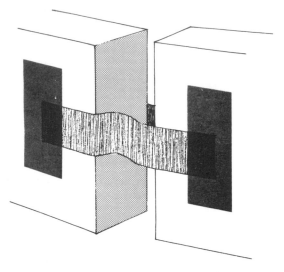

Fig. 135 Jointing the Flexibles with ribbon or tape.

In an earlier exercise (Fig. 15) we started a similar exercise with flat rectangles and we used this as a simple opportunity for measuring and calculating a length. How long was the serpent? This sort of Flexible can also be made with any number of rectangular prisms, and its final size can be computed by measuring one unit and one space.

If the flexible is to be made up of many units, the boxes will have to be collected first, and then it will be best to make them up as a number of units of two prisms joined together. The twos can then be joined as fours, and so on until the Flexible is completed. It might be interesting in school to have a Flexible serpent which stretches right round the room, or which climbs around the door frame and extends along the corridor as a welcome to visitors. It will of course have to be brightly coloured and very decorative. It might be interesting to research the patterns on various types of reptile and to reproduce some of them on the Flexibles.

The other Flexible (Fig. 134) has further shapes cut in card and added along the top as a spine. The added shapes are cut with sticking flaps and are included as part of the whole in the over-all decorative treatment, which was in this case made from overlapping pieces of torn tissue paper.

Fig. 136 A Wall of Heads.

The Flexibles illustrated are only some of the many things we can make with the rectangular prism. We might make Money Boxes by sealing them with adhesive tapes as in a later exercise. Or we might make Hand Puppets by removing one end so that the prism can be worn as a glove, and by adding features with perhaps string or wool hair. We might make Totem Pole Heads, or Hanging Heads with hair as in the previous flat exercise (Fig. 47). Or we might make a Wall of Heads (Fig. 136). It is an unusual experience to work in a classroom with a Wall of Heads brightly coloured and patterned observing everything that goes on. And there are enough rectangular prisms thrown away every day to make many different Walls of Heads.

174   The triangular prism, another basic form, is a wedge-shaped form like the two examples included in Fig. 124. It is a simple form made up with three equal sides with triangles at the top and bottom (Fig. 137). It should now be possible to draw and make the triangular prism by looking at the diagram.

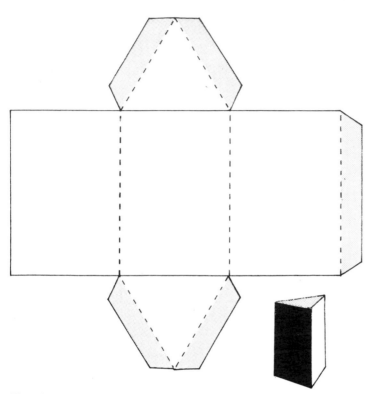

Fig. 137 The triangular prism.

Like other forms, the triangular prism is a useful form for simple free-standing experiments. It can be decorated with patterns or it can be made into particular subjects. It can be added to a rectangular or square prism as the pitched roof of a building, or because it is particularly strong, it can be used as a moving sculpture like the ones illustrated in Fig. 138.

Fig. 138 Word Maker prisms.

These triangular prisms which are attractively coloured can have a single letter on each face (Fig. 138). They can be twisted and grouped together in various ways to make words. The example illustrated is open in spacing in order to show some of the different faces of the prisms, but the forms would normally be placed together when they were being used to make words.

Fig. 139 Interlocking strip prisms.

It is interesting to make a number of decorated and lettered prisms and to devise games around them. The game can be set up with three, four or more prisms, and players in the game can move them around, making as many words as possible in a specified time—perhaps one or two minutes for each player. Unlike bought games there are no rules about playing with the Word Makers. But— also unlike bought games—we can make the rules to suit ourselves, as we can make the prisms also—and at very little cost.

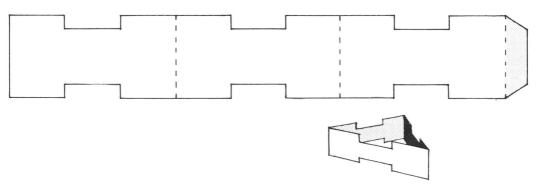

Fig. 140 The cut for the interlocking prism.

For more advanced experiments the triangular prisms, like any other form, can be made open-ended and played with in various ways. The constructions in Fig. 139 with their rich patterns of planes and angles, are each made from a sheet of thin card. This has been measured and cut into strips which have been made up into prisms. The construction of the strip involves the removal of simple sections of each face so that the prisms can be interlocking (Fig. 140). This diagram illustrates the cutting method. The prism is first established with three sides and a sticking seam, and then the middle third of each side is removed at the top and bottom as shown. For example, if the sides are each six inches long, a two-inch section can be removed from the centre. The depth of the removed portions needs to be quite shallow to make the interlocking possible. In this case the two-inch portions were cut to a depth of a half inch, which made an overlap through interlocking of one inch. The prisms illustrated were used as experiments with tone changes from light to dark and were constructed as towers—and each tower was from one sheet of flat card.

Fig. 141 Other interlocking forms are possible.

Many other interlocking multiples are possible (Fig.
141). In this example instead of triangular prisms the forms
were made hexagonal and interlocked as a tower. But this
is an exercise for those of us who can measure and cut with
confidence, and who are beginning to develop an understanding of the way forms of many different sorts can be
discovered by the deliberate manipulation of flat paper.

Tetrahedron and Pyramids

The tetrahedron is a form which has four equilateral
triangles as its sides. It is easy to construct (Fig. 142),
either with a triangular template in which every side is
equal, or by using compasses to describe arcs from corner
to corner of every side.

If sticking flaps are included as shown, the tetrahedron
can be raised as a simple pointed form (Fig. 144). In this
form every face is of equal size, and there is no specific base.
Any side can act as the base.

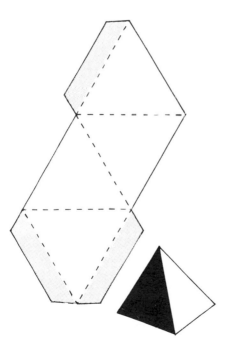

Fig. 142 The tetrahedron.

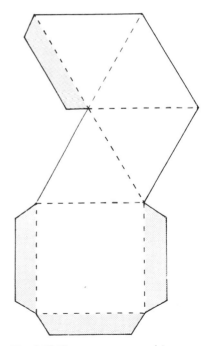

Fig. 143 The square pyramid.

Fig. 144 The tetrahedron combined as a multiple.

A form which has four equilateral triangles as its sides must have a square base (Fig. 143), and can be raised to make a four-sided pyramid, centre form in Fig. 124. Other pointed forms are possible, but with these two which are easy to construct, various multiple and decorative treatments can be explored.

A number of the forms can be assembled together. In Fig. 144 one tetrahedron carries another one on each of its four faces. The same forms are explored both as plain and decorated examples in the mobile in Fig. 145. In this case the sloping sides of the form will tend to make a curved development when a number of them are put together in a certain way. This is an interesting area for exploration.

Fig. 145 Various
arrangements of
forms are possible.

Fig. 146 Basic forms need not be developed as geometric arrangements.

But the forms need not be entirely measured and geometric. The birds in Fig. 146 have the simplest of added features, and they could be developed and exploited in many different ways with further cut or painted treatments. It is interesting to compare these birds with previous illustrations in which the same shape is used in entirely different ways. The birds are obviously of no particular species, but they have the essential features included and it should not be difficult to accept the form as a basis to work on.

To disguise the basic form more fully it would be possible to cut and add shapes all over as a surface treatment, or to add different materials. We could make highly decorative and extravagant birds on a basic form decorated with sequins or with scraps of coloured foil. We could make birds with long hanging tails like birds of paradise. If we removed the extra cut paper (except for the feet) we might make the forms into frogs. This might require a simple repositioning of the eyes and mouth. If we fixed elastic to the frog at the top, we could hold the frog down

with one hand, stretch the elastic with the other and then
release the frog. It would jump. A jumping tetrahedron—
or a jumping frog? At this stage we should be ready and
able to make the experiment for ourselves. It ought not to
be difficult to make the frog jump, which would be an
interesting and new development from the flat paper we
started with.

The Cylinder

The cylinder is the last of the basic forms we need consider.
It can be made up by rolling flat paper, and by fixing the
roll along its length, but this is hardly ever necessary. Like
the rectangular prism, there are enough cylinders thrown
out every day as waste packaging to last us throughout all
our work. It is a very rewarding form to use both in its own
right, and as a base for other shapes.

Cylinder Faces

We can begin by considering it as a base for other shapes.
The easiest cylinder to get is the cardboard core from a
toilet roll. If we take some of these and add a flat basic
shape we can make simple standing sculptures (see plate
opposite page 171). In the plain example a slot has been
cut into one end of the cylinder, and a circle of card has
been fitted into it. This is developed as a series of fun
sculptures in the other shapes. The cylinders have been
covered in patterned papers, and simple faces have been
added to the flat shapes. We can see that these flat shapes
are basic and familiar, and if we think back to our earlier
work in the use and development of shapes we will see
how the shapes work in these sculptures.

These simple funny-face sculptures can be made for
their own sake, or they might be made and used as table
decorations at a party. If they are placed carefully they can
be used to hold paper napkins, or they can be given simple
hands and made to hold labels with names showing where
the guests will sit.

184 Larger table decorations can be made on slightly heavier cylinders cut from cardboard tubes. These tubes can often be salvaged from thrown out packaging. They are used for rolling fabrics on, and for holding various sorts of printed matter. When the cylinders are thick it might be necessary to cut them into sections with a saw, but almost any kind of saw can be used.

The standing decoration (Fig. 147) shows how any simple shape can be supported in a section cut from a cylinder. We will recognize the shape and the various sorts of surface treatment, and we should be able to see many other ways of cutting and standing shapes in cylinders.

Fig. 147 The cylinder can be used as a support for any flat shape.

The triangle shape in the illustration has been cut with an extension at the base so that it can be fitted into the cylinder. This extension, which is a simple rectangle, should be an accurate fit so that the triangle will be held firmly upright. It might therefore be necessary to measure and mark this before cutting.

Any treatment of the standing shapes will allow us to use the techniques we have already practised. The clown is decorated with flat pattern and with a simple raised form repeated in the shirt frill. This form has also been cut from patterned paper (Fig. 148).

Fig. 148 Any treatment of the flat shape is possible.

If the figure is to be used as a surface decoration it will be necessary to decorate both the front and back of the shape. In this case one might include both the front and back of the clown, or even two fronts—one on each side. It is a matter of choice.

If the standing decorations are cut as simple shapes in card, and if they are fitted into heavy card cylinders, they can be made quite large; as big even as small children, and they could be very suitable for the sort of places which tend to swallow up decorations—like school and church halls and hospital wards.

Cylinders, like any other basic shape, can be made to look like anything.

Cylinder Birds

The birds in the plate opposite page 171 take the circles and triangle shape used in previous exercises. This is a symmetrical shape cut on the fold, and in this case placed in different positions on decorated toilet roll cores: at the top, sideways or at the bottom. Simple wings, crests and legs have been fixed to the cylinders to complete the birds. They can be hung at any angle. They are easy to make, and if we use toilet roll cores and salvaged wrapping paper, they are very cheap.

They are also very suitable for room and home decorations because they are very light and can be hung with a fine thread pinned to the ceiling with a dressmaker's pin. With such a decoration the only damage to even the smartest ceiling would be a series of pinholes, which would be quite invisible to the naked eye.

It is sometimes possible just to make one creature like this, and to pay particular care to the way it is coloured and decorated. It can then become a rather special toy with its own name perhaps. We will often grow much fonder of something we make ourselves than of many of the expensive toys which we sometimes might not really want at all.

If we can make Cylinder Birds we must also be able to make fish. The fish in Fig. 149 are made in a similar way to the birds. Toilet roll or kitchen towel cores are used again for the body. In the fish illustrated, the mouth and eye section is cut as one piece of paper. This is a simple strip which fits over the cylinder and has a large eye at each end. The eyes can be fixed with glue or staples at the sides of the

Cylinder Fish

Fig. 149 They may become swimming fish.

188 cylinder, and the strip of paper between them can be drawn as a mouth.

The tail cut double on a folded paper can have a projection which fits into the end of the cylinder. This makes it an easy fixture. Fins and other features in various shapes can be fixed wherever they will add to the effect.

The cylinder fish will, of course, make excellent mobiles, and will swim around all the time once they are balanced and hung. There are many different patterns and shapes possible.

The Flexibles (Figs. 150 and 151) are similar to the flexibles suggested as an earlier exercise with rectangular prisms. The first one is made up with a number of cylinders connected together with ribbon. The ribbons have been fixed

Cylinder Flexibles

Fig. 150 Cylinder Flexible can be joined together with ribbon . . .

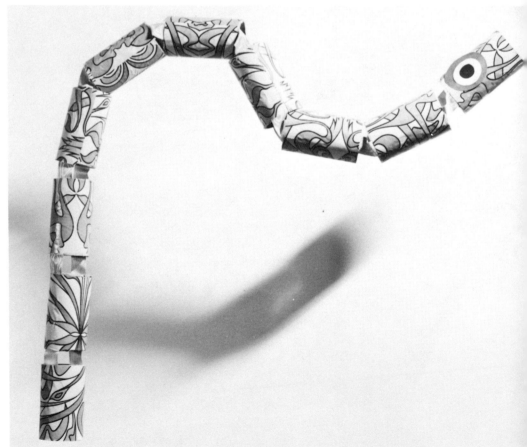

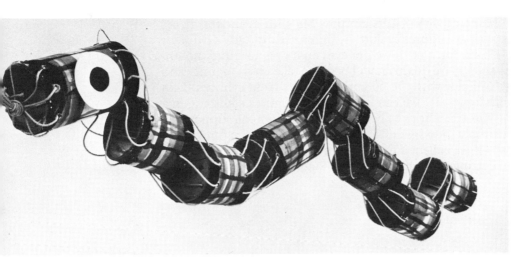

Fig. 151 . . . or with string.

first, and the cylinders have then been decorated, hiding the fixture.

The second Flexible is connected with strings passed through holes pierced in each cylinder. It can be twisted and turned in any direction, and could be made any length.

Cylinder Flexibles are fun to make and use. The class boa-constrictor could grow a new section each week, and its growth could be measured and recorded. During the school holidays it could be coiled away in the cupboard to hibernate. It could shed one skin at the beginning of a new term and could be given a completely new one with fresh colours and patterns.

The Flexibles could take many shapes. There are serpents and dragons and underwater monsters waiting to be made. There are giant eels and spotted congers and, most important of all, there is an unlimited supply of cylinders to be had entirely free of charge. In the summer, instead of keeping all our work inside, we might varnish the Flexibles and put them in the nearest tree, or perhaps even coil them along the school railings. There is certainly no rule which says that all the work we do must be kept inside a building. And at this point, if we have been working with some of our friends in the class, there should be very little space left to hang or coil an enormously long Cylinder Flexible.

Many other subjects are possible with cylinders. Faces as puppets, figures as skittles, animals in a circus; a cylinder is a basic form until we put eyes on it or a nose and mouth. As soon as we do this it will begin to take on an identity and we can play with the potential. We can hang cylinder faces with long hair; we can have cylinder figures standing on a flat surface. They can be kings, knights, football supporters, or simple friendly dolls. There is no limit to the fun we can have if we collect a few cylinders and if we have some skill in cutting and manipulating paper.

Strip Modelling

There is a long established method of pattern making with paper in which strips are cut in contrasting colours and then woven together like fabric. This will make an interesting flat arrangement of paper, and will provide many opportunities for experiment with colour. It is a simple technique which can be started with three strips, two vertical and one across these in an over-and-under arrangement. A fourth strip can be added to the horizontal, and then another vertical can be introduced, and so on as the weaving is developed from the centre outwards.

The paper strip, which can be bent and folded into many forms, is worth looking at. It can be cut to any thickness, although a one-inch strip (2·5 cm) is a good starting size. The strips can be cut with scissors along drawn lines or they can be cut with a knife and straight edge. Even better, they can be cut on a guillotine if there is one available and if its careful use is allowed.

Fig. 152 Free-standing strip sculptures.

Strip Sculptures

The strip sculptures (Fig. 152) relate very much to some of the work we considered earlier with cut and applied shapes. In each of the examples illustrated the outer frame was measured and made up as an open-ended prism; square or triangular. The original strip and subsequent added forms were all measured to include a sticking flap where it would be needed.

After the outer forms were made up, inset shapes were measured and made and then stuck with clear cellulose adhesive. The forms, which were made slightly smaller than this page, were filled with inset shapes until there was no adequate space left to work in. They were made as practical exercises in measurement, and were then used as free-standing sculptures. In some cases they were hung as mobiles because the change in light and dark tone contrast and the cast shadows were particularly effective as the forms moved. This sort of work with strip sculptures based on measured and precise units is again an opportunity for the mathematically minded. The care and patience required might infuriate some of us, but these of course should leave the exercise alone.

Fig. 153 Strip sculptures can be made in simple forms.

Fig. 154 One form can be variously exploited with strip sculpture.

We know now that the cylinder is a basic form, and although it is easy to find already made up, it is a form easily modelled in strip sculpture. After cutting a strip, preferably in good quality and fairly thick paper, it can be gently modelled into one or into a number of rolls as shown in Fig. 153. The forms, which should be as accurate as possible, should be neither too tight nor too loose. It is a matter of appreciating what the paper can be made to do. When the rolls are made up they should be stapled at once, otherwise they will just spring open when they are put down.

A number of rolls made up as shown can be put together in various ways. In the vertical arrangement they were stapled to the strip on alternate sides. The closer arrangement is of a number of rolls stapled together. This could be extended to a much larger form, although the weight factor would have to be considered or the form might become distorted and ugly.

There are many different arrangements possible with strip rolls. When a number of rolls are made together and then used as units for a bigger arrangement, the light and shadow contrasts will be effective, and the forms will make simple but attractive decorations. They could be made less serious if—to go back to earlier exercises—they could be hung with a face at the top, turning freely—or even at the bottom.

Other developments of the strips might be explored. The square prisms in the mobile Fig. 154 are patterned on the outer edges with strips developed in different ways. These and others like them can be developed freehand, or they can be made as measuring exercises and folded on the working surfaces at the appropriate places before being fixed to the hanging form.

As an example of a more complex exercise a pattern of strip rectangular prisms has been arranged in Fig. 155 to make an all-over form of its own. This can be understood by a close scrutiny of the illustration, but this and other similar exercises are again for those who get satisfaction from working in this special sort of way.

It is more fun and easier with the strips to make forms like the fish in Fig. 156 or the owls in Fig. 157. These are simple strip versions of work we have already tried in various different ways. The outer shape of the fish is made with a single strip secured at the tail. A fixture can be made

Fig. 155 Strip sculpture making its own form.

Fig. 156 Strip sculpture can suggest simple forms . . .

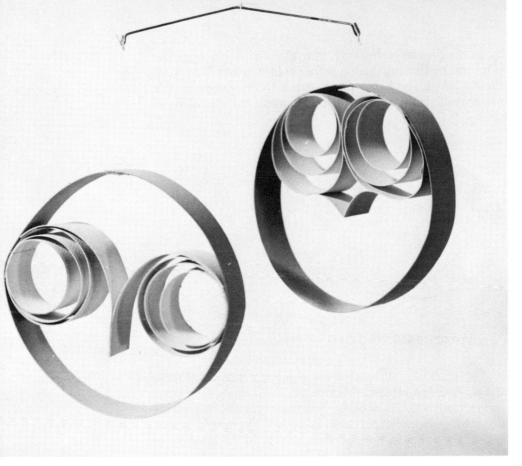

Fig. 157 . . . with various identities.

198   by cutting exactly halfway into the strips on opposite sides and by slotting them together as in Fig. 158. The form should be pinched to a point at the front. Other simple patterns of strips can be made and inset into the forms as shown.

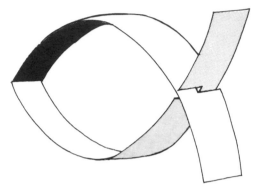

Fig. 158 Slotting and fixing the strip forms.

The examples illustrated are again an introduction to the potential of a technique. Like the techniques developed in previous exercises Strip Sculpture can be a starting point for personal experiment and play. The results which we achieve should be looked at closely in an attempt to understand them, and should lead us on to other new developments. The strips can be contrasted in colour but they should be of the same width in any work. A single sheet of paper will make a large number of strips, which in turn will make many different strip forms.

Christmas

After all the exercises, Christmas and the preparation for it, or any other party or festive occasion, must be an opportunity for us to play in a very purposeful way. We can make our own very real contributions to the occasion and we will not have to rely entirely on stores and their factory-made goods.

Any fun which we might have had when we were trying some of the earlier exercises will have extended our ability to use paper. Every cut we made, every fold and every fixture will have meant that we were touching and looking at the material and that, although we might not have been aware of it, our personal skill was growing.

The practical results as our work developed might have been very different, but the techniques we used will have been the same, and now that we have them we will be able to apply them on any future occasion. These, and our continuing willingness to experiment with them will make it possible for us to do many things with paper.

We might illustrate this by taking a simple creative exercise and seeing now how we are able to apply our different techniques in various ways. We can begin with one subject.

Christmas Trees

The simplest Christmas tree (Fig. 159) is a flat paper shape with a projection at the bottom which is inserted into part of a cylinder. This is a technique which we can use to make the tree stand. The shape, which is a simple cut-out with a number of symmetrical points can be related to its starting point as a rectangle. We can see how the template from which it is cut has been made by folding the rectangle. It will also be seen that the template has been used throughout this part of the exercise.

Fig. 159 The simplest Christmas tree starts from known techniques.

To the right of the plain shape we can see the first development. The cylindrical base has been decorated, and an applied decoration cut in simple shapes has been added to the surface. The applied decoration is in paper collage, but it might equally as well have been in any material: fabric, wool, wood shavings, straw, foil—there are many easily obtained things which we might experiment with. In some cases it might be necessary to dye the material or to paint over it after sticking it to the surface, but we are free to make our own decisions about applied colour and pattern.

If we choose to decorate the tree with colours rather than with applied shapes we can use any medium we like. We can obviously paint—and there are many different types of paint available, especially today with the development of polymer and acrylic colours. We can use ink— with a brush, with a pen or drinking straw, with a stick or a string to move it about on the surface. We can use wax crayons as colours, or we can use them as a resist medium —applying the wax in places and then painting over the whole surface with inks or dyes, which will be resisted by the wax. We can print the surface of the tree with a stick, or with a finger, or with a piece of vegetable, or with any suitable found shape: a cork or a piece of card. There are more ways of decorating the flat shape than it is possible to describe here. And we all have our own choice to make.

Our choice of paper for the shape itself will depend on how we intend to work on it. We may choose a stiff coloured paper, or we may start with a thin white card which we will dye. It is easy to apply dye with a sponge, and useful to colour a few sheets of card at the same time, packing them away flat when they are dry, for use in the future. We can start with white card which we can buy, or we can collect and cut up boxes. We might even start with brown card from large cartons which can also be effectively dyed.

In the two remaining trees in this illustration the decoration uses again the technique of cutting and applying shapes to a surface. In the example on the left the shapes have been cut in a continuous strip and have been patterned on their surfaces. The strip has been applied with raised forms along its length, so that it will have contrasting shadows on its surface and will also cast shadows of its own.

In the similarly treated example on the right, the shapes in the applied strip have also been surface cut before being stuck, so that there is a decorative effect between the spaces and the shadows. Since these shapes have been surface cut they have been deliberately made larger.

In Fig. 160 the same shape is exploited in different ways. In the examples shown vertical folds are introduced into the original shapes made with the template, and in some cases a number of folded shapes are put together. This sort of development can be related back to the treatment of the stars in a previous exercise (Fig. 110).

In the front centre example the flat shape is folded on two creases, one side towards the front and one to the back. In the other examples in this illustration there are various multiple arrangements similar to those tried in previous exercises.

In one of the examples shown, the points of the tree have been partly curled by surface scraping to add to the effect, and to demonstrate the simple application of this technique. This and the other trees could be surface decorated like the one shown.

Fig. 160 The tree can be further exploited.

We have arrived by the application of some of the techniques we know at a simple three-dimensional Christmas tree, having started with flat paper. We can now experiment deliberately with a suitable three-dimensional form which we already know.

To make the form in Fig. 161 we might have to refer back to an earlier exercise (Fig. 142), although in this case the triangles are deliberately made with sides longer than the base. If we can cut and make this form we can decorate it as we like, again using some of the techniques we have learned. There are as many different ways of decorating the surfaces of the form, illustrated here with simple

Fig. 161 It can be made as a deliberate form.

stripes and circles, as there are ways of decorating the flat shapes in the previous developments.

From the techniques used in our earlier work we might decide to use a cut surface treatment before making up the form in Fig. 162. The cuts will, of course, be made on the sides only and not on the base. The simplest cut, as we have seen previously, is the v-cut which is made with two straight knife cuts. The cut pieces can be raised, like the example illustrated, on a fold; or they can be curled. A cut and raised surface can also have simple applied decoration which will be specially effective in this exercise if shapes are cut from coloured and patterned foil.

Fig. 162 The form can have cut surface treatment . . .

204   We also considered in a previous exercise how a surface
can be made more interesting by the addition of folded
shapes (Fig. 85). In Fig. 163 the tree form is treated in this
way. In the example on the left the shapes have been curled
slightly before being stuck to the tree, and have had spots
of colour added. In the other example circles cut in a contrasting colour have been folded twice so that they can be
stuck at the flat part and can have both sides raised. In both
instances a number of the shapes could be cut in one operation with the paper folded. The possibilities of surface

Fig. 163 . . . or cut and applied shapes.

shapes and colours to be explored.

It might be interesting to note that in this illustration the trees are stuck on inverted paper cups and not on cylinders. This is another useful source of salvaged and usable material.

Some people might like their Christmas trees more open, but this again is a possible variation which might be explored in paper.

If we take a flat triangle of paper, and if we fold it vertically through the centre we can cut into the fold with parallel cuts (Fig. 164). The arrow indicates the way the cuts must be made, through the fold, parallel to the base, at equal intervals, and stopping short of the outer edges of the triangle.

After making the cuts we can pull alternate strips from the fold to the opposite side as shown. The folds can be pressed into place where the strips are turned at the ends of the cuts (Fig. 164A).

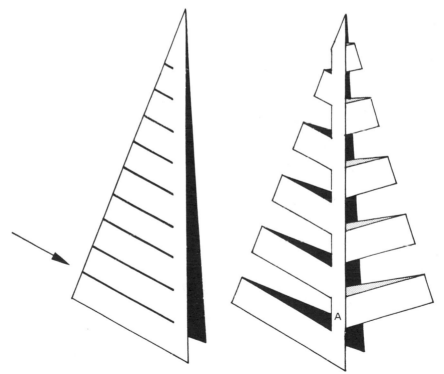

Fig. 164 The form can be cut and folded from a flat triangle.

206 The tree-like form which results from this method of cutting and folding can be supported on a cylinder of card (Fig. 165). It makes a simple home-made tree which can be decorated in many ways. But it is not necessary at this point to suggest ways of decorating a paper form. The opening of a triangle like this makes it visually interesting. Slight variations in the angle of the fold can be achieved through changing the angle of the cut, but this is again a matter for experiment and personal decision.

Fig. 165 Flat folded trees can be supported on a cylinder.

Triangles cut like this in brightly coloured papers might be hung with faces at the top, so that they would suggest a body. Or they might be hung with faces under them so that the decoration would look like a funny face wearing a moving hat.

There will be some people perhaps who after these suggestions will still prefer their Christmas trees to be the actual thing, although various sorts of artificial trees are common today. If there is a preference for one thing then there is obviously no reason to interfere with it. We can all please ourselves when we play. If we do not want to experiment with paper Christmas trees we can find other opportunities: party hats—the triangles might make very good party hats; table decorations—circus animals, clowns, angels. There are so many shapes to explore.

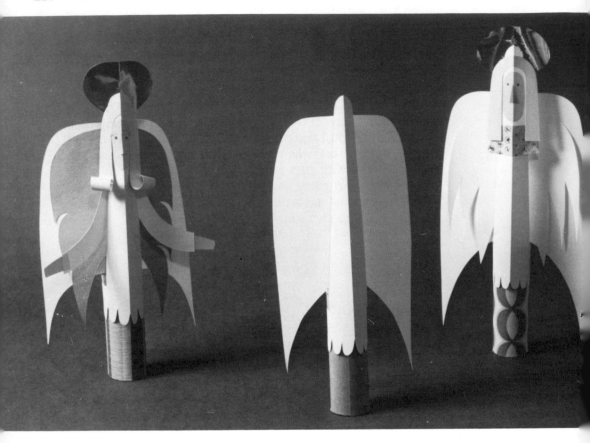

Fig. 166 The techniques can be used for other Christmas shapes.

Angel

The angel in Fig. 166 stands on a piece of a cylinder. The symmetrical wing shape drops into the cylinder because it has a section included at the bottom. We know this technique from previous exercises. The thin body shape has a band at the base which can be wrapped round the top of the cylinder. This shape (Fig. 167), being cut on the fold and partly retaining the fold in its made-up state, is strengthened, as we know, by the technique so that although it is slender it will stand upright.

Additional features, including arms and a simple face, should be well within the ability of any of us. We might put a second wing in contrasting colour against the first one, and we will certainly want to decorate the cylinder at the base.

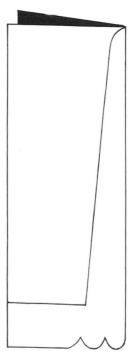

Fig. 167 The cut for the angel shape.

The angels can be free-standing or, like so many other subjects cut in paper, they can be hung at various angles and in many different arrangements.

Greeting Cards   For birthdays and Christmases we will need cards for our friends. It is easy to go out and buy them, but there is something very special about receiving a card made by the sender. When we can cut and arrange paper shapes we can make many different cards.

If we receive a card we are usually able to stand it up on a shelf or a mantelpiece. Or when we buy cards to send we usually assume that they will be printed on folded card.

It is never really necessary to spend money on cards. Because they are relatively small we can use the scraps from previous exercises to make them. We can certainly make some of the hanging shapes suggested earlier, and we can send these through the post. It is often a mistake to try to draw and paint cards. The control and skill needed are very special. But by this stage we should have a very adequate ability to cut and play with shapes.

Fig. 168 Greeting cards can be different.

The cards in Fig. 168 are simple folded shapes with faces added: cats—and they are all wearing party hats made from scraps picked up from the studio floor. The party hats, which are simple enough to cut, make the cats festive, and a card does not have to have a square top. It could be curved like a cat, and there must be many other subjects which would look right for the occasion if, like the cats, they were cut wearing attractive party hats.

If we extend the folding technique we might consider making two folds, as in the example on the right. In which case we would get three faces to decorate or hats to make. In the example shown the cut edge treatments help to make the card interesting and to establish a simple character. It might be interesting to try making a greeting card which was an even longer line of lions, or smiling or contentedly sleeping animals of our own choice.

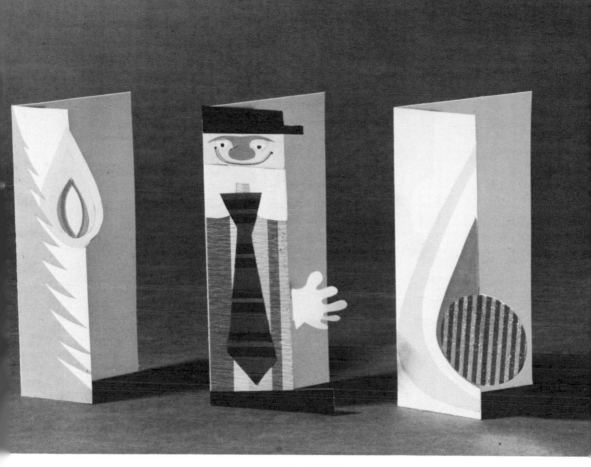

Fig. 169 The cards can be cut on one edge.

With more normal single fold cards in which the picture statement is at the front we can still experiment with cutting rather than drawing. In the examples illustrated (Fig. 169) the front of a single fold card is changed with cut edge treatments. This must be kept deliberately simple so that the cutting is possible in a few strokes. The cuts (Fig. 170) will separate the front of the card from the back. They will allow us to establish simple subjects with added paper shapes on the front surfaces, and the simpler the subject the more effective the card is likely to be.

The double fold cards (Fig. 171) illustrate a way of making the material work for us. In each case the centre section behind the front two is decorated, either with a patterned paper or by hand, and the cuts on the edges are made to suggest a shape when the sides are folded across the front.

Fig. 170 Various cuts are possible in the folded card.

Fig. 171 The double fold cut will make a variety of cards.

The tree in the centre card is no more than a series of v-cuts in both edges of the card. Simple cuts like this must be well within the reach of any of us. In the same way the tree on the right is suggested merely by cutting one shape from one side and then using this as a template to cut a similar shape on the other.

Like so much of our work with paper, interesting and effective greeting cards become possible when we know how to use simple devices and techniques. The Christmas tree, the angel and the cards are all examples of how techniques—all of them previously considered in earlier exercises—can be experimented with in a particular situation. But the examples shown are intended only as suggestions. They illustrate only the beginning and not the whole of the potential.

Money Boxes

At Christmas and party times, however, we might need more than a few bits of paper and some confident techniques. We might need some more decorated papers; and although we can make some presents in paper, we might need to buy others.

Most of the things suggested in this book are anything but useful. They might be fun objects, and they might be attractive and colourful, but it would mostly be very difficult to find any real and convincing use for them.

Money Boxes are different. They really are useful.

The simplest of these is the well-known rectangular prism, a box sealed up with adhesive tape and covered with decorative paper. Like any sort of money box the slot at the top must be large enough to take money, but difficult to get it back from.

Maze Money Boxes

The other examples in the illustration are variations on the simple money box. These Maze Money Boxes will require a little more skill in construction, but they are interesting to make. A number of basic forms, in this case rectangular prisms or cylinders, can be put together in visually interesting ways. If the arrangement is planned before they are fixed together, holes can be cut at the right places so that coins will be able to drop from one box to the next—and on to the next and the next. When the forms are finally stuck and taped as a maze, the holes will be at the

Fig. 172 Husband and Wife Money Boxes.

meeting points on the inside and will not be seen. There will be only one slot at the top for the money to pass through. It is interesting to shake any saved coins down through the various compartments of the maze, and to know how they are passing from one form to the next.

The example of the Maze Money Box made from cylinders illustrates another use for toilet roll cores. In these the open ends are sealed with flat discs of card and adhesive tape. There are openings cut between the cylinders where they join, but again these cannot be seen when the cylinders are taped together and decorated.

The Husband and Wife Money Boxes (Fig. 172) are a development on an earlier exercise in which simple face shapes were slotted into cylinders. In this instance the cylinders are sealed at the top and bottom, and the flat face shapes are stuck on so that coins inserted into the slot at the mouth will fall into the cylinder. This is possible if a flat rectangular section is cut from the top edge of the cylinder so that it will coincide with the mouth. Strips of adhesive tape will hold the face to the cylinder and can be used to strengthen the seal at the top—keeping the saved money secure.

Flappers

Finally for those of us who like to hear the chink of coins saved there is the Flapper. These are bird shapes with wide wings which will flap up and down when the form is moved.

The body shape can be a cylinder or any other basic form, or as in the illustration in Fig. 173 it can be a paper cup with the opening sealed—or better still two paper cups joined together. If the body is sealed a slot can be cut at the top for the coins.

To make the coins chink the Flappers must be suspended on elastic and not on thread, so that they can be bounced up and down to make the happy sound. When this is done the coins will chink together and the wings will flap, and we will know the money is safe. The Flappers will also, as the weight of the saved coins gets heavier, hang lower and lower because the elastic will stretch. The lower they hang the more we will have saved—either for ourselves—or better still, as a collection for one of the many deserving causes around us.

216 It is as much fun to watch a Flapper in the classroom flying lower and lower in a good cause as it is to make one. Some paper cups, off-cuts of coloured paper, glue and elastic—at this point in the book we should have a firm grip on the techniques necessary to make the Flappers. They are very easy.

Fig. 173 Flappers—the chink of coins saved.

There are many different suggestions in this book for playing with paper, but when we have reached the Flappers we might pause to consider going our own ways. Some of us will use our techniques to go in one direction, searching out new subjects and forms to play with, and some of us will go in another.

This is not meant to be a final or total statement on the potential of the material. The intention is to add some new ideas and methods of working to those suggested in earlier titles in the series. Paper and card are simple materials. They are cheap and usually easy to get, and they are both colourful and attractive.

If we have time and the beginnings of an interest, and if we are not too serious about the results, we can have fun. Like any other sort of play, paper play is fun—but it can also be creative and satisfying if we can make some of the things suggested in this book. Or better still—if we can discover and make new things for ourselves as we go on playing with paper in our own particular ways.